WIND

G. M. Glaskin

WINDOWS OF THE MIND

The Christos Experience

ARROW BOOKS

ARROW BOOKS LTD
3 Fitzroy Square, London W1

An imprint of the Hutchinson Publishing Group

London Melbourne Sydney Auckland
Wellington Johannesburg Cape Town
and agencies throughout the world

First published by Wildwood House Ltd 1974
Arrow edition 1975

The authors and publishers gratefully acknowledge permission to reproduce extracts from copyright material which appear on the following pages:
pp. 73–4, from *The House on the Strand*, by Daphne du Maurier (Victor Gollancz, London, 1969)
pp. 132–3, from the *Encyclopedia Britannica* (Encyclopedia Britannica, Chicago, 1961) © *Encyclopedia Britannica* 1961.
pp. 203–4, from *Return to the Stars*, by Erich von Daniken (Souvenir Press, London 1970)

Made and printed in Great Britain
by The Anchor Press Ltd
Tiptree, Essex

ISBN 0 09 910510 1

Acknowledgments

First and foremost acknowledgment must be made to the founder of the 'The Christos Experiment' and editor of *Open Mind* Publications at Mahogany Creek in Western Australia, a few pages (15 to 18) in one of which (Booklet No. 5, May/June 1971) introduced me to the procedure which has resulted in this book.

'This is none other but the house of God,
and this is the gate of heaven.'

Genesis, xxviii, 17

For JOY and RAY
who first gave me the Christos Experience

and for LEO VAN DE PAS
who witnessed and assisted with
each and every experiment

Warning

The procedure given in this book, which makes it possible to dream while one is fully awake, and which possibly even reveals past lives and/or future events, is not to be treated lightly, and particularly not as some new and intriguing party game, exciting as the experience may be. As in dreams experienced during normal necessary sleep, nightmares and unpleasant experiences can and do occur, which may cause distress to some subjects despite their being able to terminate the experiment at any time, something not possible when they have a nightmare during normal sleep. Such unpleasant experiences have occurred when the experiment was carried out in both New York and London—without the author's presence, of course. On the other hand, most experimentees have expressed their astonishment at what a pleasant, marvellous, experience it is; a considerable number, incredulous as they may have been beforehand, have claimed to have benefited greatly from it both psychologically and through revelations of future events as well as of experiences indisputably before their present lifetimes.

GERALD M. GLASKIN, *author*
WILDWOOD HOUSE, *publishers*

Chapter One

Have we *only* the one life? Or do we have several, travelling—or migrating—from one 'incarnation' to another? My own encounter with this possibility began, as do so many things in life, purely by chance.

I had to idle away a few moments in the home of friends of mine—let's call them Joy and Ray for this publication—before we were all to go out. And so I picked up a magazine lying near by and, intrigued a little by its title of *The Christos Experiment—Introductory Principles*, I just as idly leafed through its seventy pages of offset typescript, a form of print which in itself showed the magazine to be of small circulation.

What was the Christos Experiment? At a glance it seemed to be something to do with yet another of those numerous religious-cum-philosophical bodies—bodies with a few devoted followers who appear to many outsiders to be fanatical, even to the extent of being 'cranks' or 'a bit soft in the head'. This, I saw, was booklet No. 5 for May/June 1971 and its editor lived in what is more a sub-rural than a sub-urban locality of my city of Perth in its remote State of Western Australia. It was a place called Mahogany Creek; its nearest post office was a few miles away in a small township called Mundaring. There was nothing urbane about this magazine as if it had been published in, say, London, or Paris, or somewhere in the United States.

Still leafing through the pages, I was confronted by such sub-headings as 'Preparations for the New Age', 'Soul Contact', 'Reincarnation' and 'The Seven Bodies of Man'. One section, 'Introduction to Expansion of Consciousness', described a method to 'lift one's consciousness from the Astral level to the

Mental and Buddhic levels', followed by 'Analysis of the Self' and 'Meditation'.

During the years, I had seen all too much of this kind of literature and none of it had ever managed to do more than arouse a very temporary curiosity and a half-hearted interest, which soon failed to carry any conviction. This booklet did appear to be much better written than most; in fact, when I read a few lines here and there, it became obvious that it was very well written indeed by someone of indubitable education and intelligence. And so, as I still had a few more minutes to wait for Joy and Ray to finish their dressing, I read on.

'Etheric or Vital Body', 'Chakras', 'Planes', 'Astral Body', 'The Mind or Mental Body', 'Causal Body or Higher Self', 'Buddhic Body', 'Atmaic and Monadic Bodies', 'Atmaic Consciousness': like the simple but effective line drawing used as an illustration on the cover, it all smacked rather of the Middle East or India, and of the various religions I had encountered during ten years of living and working in multiracial Singapore.

I was about to put the book down, feeling it offered nothing new, when a heading seemed to leap out at me: 'A METHOD TO REMEMBER PAST LIVES'. Really? I couldn't have been more sceptical. But at that moment Ray appeared in the room to say that they wouldn't be much longer, followed a little later by Joy to apologize for being late. Joy saw what I was reading, stopped, then said, 'I'd like you to read that. It sounds absolutely fascinating. A friend of mine tried it and says that it not only works, it's incredible.'

'Do I know the friend?' I inquired, still sceptical.

I did, and it was someone whose integrity I respected very much. And so there was nothing else for it but to read the entire piece and, having read it, to try the experiment out for myself a few evenings later.

The author of 'A Method to Remember Past Lives' claimed success almost without exception: not only did the experiences reveal 'past lives' (prior to one's present 'incarnation'), but they indicated solutions to problems in one's present life or 'incarnation'. The method seemed quite simple and did not involve any inherently dangerous procedures such as hypnotism or even prolonged auto-suggestion, so we agreed to try it—on me.

To begin with, the person being 'run' (this is an American term for the technique) was to undergo a few 'preliminary mental exercises' while lying flat on his back on the floor, his eyes closed, and with a cushion supporting his head and his shoes removed. The last requirement was said to be 'very necessary' as 'before anything can start, the person's ankles and feet must be massaged for a few minutes to loosen them'—quite a pleasurable and relaxing feeling in itself. Then, while one person is massaging the feet, another uses the outer edge of a clenched hand to massage the centre of the forehead, or 'the third eye area', with a circular motion. This was to be done 'vigorously for several minutes', until the head was 'really buzzing'.

My head didn't actually buzz, but I did experience an agreeable and yet confusing feeling, for the mind could not concentrate simultaneously on both the areas of the body receiving all this pleasant attention. I found that I could concentrate on one or the other, but not on both simultaneously, although I must admit that while I concentrated on the strangely stimulating yet relaxing effect of the massage in one area I had a very secondary awareness of its effect in the other. Within a few minutes—I think two or three—there was a distinct change: I was no longer aware of it either on the forehead or at my ankles, but was succumbing to a new feeling of my mind being both with*in* and with*out* (meaning outside) the confines of my skull; not only that, but it appeared to be both a conscious and subconscious feeling. And there was no doubt about it, I was indeed completely relaxed. I might have been not so much just lying on the floor as *floating* above it.

Then the 'mental exercises' were begun. Joy had the book of instructions, which of course I had previously read and so was somewhat prepared for them. I was to visualize myself growing two inches taller. Actually I think 'longer' would have been a better word than 'taller', for two reasons: firstly, I was, of course, horizontal instead of vertical; and secondly, I was to visualize this 'growth' first, not where one might expect it, in the head and upper body, but through the soles of the feet. I giggled, I'm afraid; I just couldn't believe it could work. I have lived for several years now on the products of what is evidently a fairly good imagination, but I just couldn't conceive of ever being able to imagine growing taller through my feet! As it was, it was as much as I could do to suppress my idiotic giggle.

And then the 'growth', or the first of several growths, did indeed happen. Although my eyes were firmly closed, I could actually *see* my legs at the ankles. (These were no longer being rubbed; and the rubbing of my forehead had stopped as well.) I saw them stretch out and so push my feet two inches from where they had previously been, at all events in my visualization of them. Asked if I had grown, I answered quite seriously, and I suppose even incredulously, yes. I was then told to visualize my legs shrinking back to their normal length. It took a few moments, but soon I was able to say, 'Yes', I was back to my normal height or length again. I could not only visualize it, I could feel it. At the same time it occurred to me that there was really nothing very remarkable about it; it was merely a rather simple and elementary exercise of the imagination. I was 'stretched out' and brought back again, several more times, through my feet.

Then the process was changed and the 'stretching' done through my head, again several times. This I found very much easier, though whether that was because I was becoming accustomed to the procedure, or because it seemed more 'usual' to grow through the head rather than the feet, I cannot even now determine. Possibly it was due to a combination of both.

Was this all? Far from it. My concentration had to revert to growing through the feet again; but this time not just two inches, but twelve. And once more I was soon astounded to find that I was both visualizing and feeling this incredible growth.

After this, I grew through the head. I then repeated the whole procedure, but now for twenty-four inches. I was told that, when asked if I had 'grown' this considerable amount, my answer 'yes' came in less than a minute, just as the instructions (which I was shown afterwards) said that it should.

Next stage—stretching twenty-four inches through both feet and head at the same time. I didn't laugh this time, though I did have an inclination to do so, for at first I felt that I was indeed growing twenty-four inches again through my head, but that my legs were withdrawing at the same time. Yet it must have been only a matter of seconds before this confusion ceased, for I was again told afterwards that it was under a minute before I said that I had managed this growth in both directions. I had also lost all urge to giggle, though my scepticism was still with me. Very much so.

Then came what seemed the impossible. I had to expand all over, to grow in all directions, much like some giant balloon. I tried. Nothing happened. I tried again. I was just going to say I couldn't when to my surprise I found myself doing, or feeling that I was doing, just exactly that—expanding in all directions so that I could see myself, or at least feel as though I were seeing myself, becoming an enormous globe.

From this point something went wrong so far as I was concerned. I was now supposed to start 'seeing' things, but the things I was to see were to be 'suggested' to me by Joy (or the person 'running' me). I should have been told to visualize my own front door and, when I could see it, to describe it in detail. Then I should have been instructed to take myself to the top of the roof of my house and look down and 'see', and describe everything I could see from that vantage point. I missed this part. In her excitement at my having at last managed to 'expand', Joy asked me if I had started to see anything instead of merely telling me to visualize my front door.

I could indeed see something, though it was very vague and rather brown and murky—I was looking up at the spreading tops of pillars in some dimly-lit cathedral. This didn't strike me as being in the least unusual; at any time of the day you can close your eyes and all kinds of images, patterns, symbols or pictures will 'come into vision'. At first I considered my cathedral pillars as no more than some kind of auto-suggested image or a form of self-induced daydream. When I was asked, I described the picture; and at the same time it not only seemed to become clearer, though still of a rather dim interior, but either I was ascending towards the ceiling or it was descending towards me. Then I was sure that it was the former. I was ascending. I was floating. I was even beginning to move rather rapidly now, though with a steadiness, even a serenity, in the speed of the motion.

This, a separate part of my consciousness told me, was perhaps the beginning of the 'astral travelling' that should have been induced by visualizing my house and its surroundings from the roof and immediately afterwards from about five hundred feet above it. On a later occasion, Ray was to follow the sequence precisely; but in my first experience, I was way ahead of where I should have been.

It was an eerie feeling, though one that is experienced quite frequently in dreams when sleeping. Now, however, I was conscious—and conscious, what is more, of still lying on the living-room floor in Ray and Joy's house while at the same time gliding up towards my cathedral ceiling. Both experiences were perfectly clear. I was two separate yet undeniably connected identities.

Then the roof of the cathedral appeared to open and I could see the sun shining fitfully through varying layers of cloud moving slowly across the sky. Colour began to seep into my 'vision', especially the luminous golds at the edges of clouds. Now I was not just merely gliding, I was soaring, and I said so.

Joy was uncertain of what to do now. She realized that I had somehow skipped well ahead of the course the 'run' should have taken. She should have had me visualizing my surroundings from five hundred feet above my house by night as well as by day, and then by day again. Only after that had been accomplished should I 'travel', in the safety of daylight so that I wouldn't 'collide' with anything in the dark, and also so that I wouldn't 'land' in dangerous circumstances from some 'past life'. This, the book said, had sometimes happened with some experimenters: one person had landed upside down in the ocean; he couldn't swim and not only went into hysteria but made all the motions of a man drowning as well; another had 'landed' in a sixteenth-century tavern in some alien country, only to have the other men there set on him and cut his throat—and his *actual* throat instantly developed a red line across it as he tried to protect himself with his hands. (I must remind you that this is only hearsay so far as I am concerned.)

Joy, realizing I was 'off' already, attempted to bring me back to taking the normal course by asking me to visualize my door. She should have instructed me to visualize my sunlit earth and to land my feet soundly on it, but this I had already done.

And there *was* a door before me. It was not my own door, however, as the others soon found when I was asked to describe it. It was a double door, arched to a point, church-fashion, and made of vertical slats of wood three to four inches wide and almost as thick, but roughly made, not straight as though sawn at a mill, and bound together by heavy but roughly-made hasps in simple curving patterns.

These doors were set in enormous and immensely thick walls built from large and rough-hewn stones, grimed and pitted with age and sun and desert dust. The doors were about ten feet high and three to four feet wide (the two together). What was odd about them was that they were the only doors, the only opening whatsoever, in the huge expanse of wall. Not only that: as I clearly described at the time, the left door opened outwards and the right door inwards.

I was told to go inside, and so I prepared myself to enter. Inside it was pitch black. My eyes had to become accustomed to the dark after the bright sunshine outside, where I still stood. What's more, I could *feel* the heat of the sun on my back.

'What kind of building is it?' Joy asked.

'Some kind of a mausoleum,' I told them. 'Or a temple. Something like that.'

'Are you afraid?'

'No.'

'Will you go inside?'

'Yes.'

And I *went* inside. It was immediately very cold. The black of the darkness spread all round and above me, to an enormous height. The air was dank. The sun fell a little way inside the doorway, but not very far; and my shadow, long and narrow, blocked out most of what was before me—a stone floor. The floor was not only cold but wet; water was trickling down a groove carved in the stone floor, a groove that ran from a bowl-shaped indenture in the centre of what I could now see was a circular interior. And this groove gradually widened from a few inches at the centre of the floor to almost the width of the door, to which it ran, carrying outside the moisture which dripped from the ceiling. It was really a shallow open drain.

Around the walls were stone sarcophagi. They were not ornately carved, but on the contrary, rather plain. Several of them, I knew—knew without being 'told'—contained the bodies of my predecessors, but predecessors by election and not by familial descent of birth. My own sarcophagus was awaiting me, for when I should die, and there were others in a long line round the huge circumference wall, awaiting those who would succeed me.

I did not have to be told all this by 'someone' appearing in the vision; I instinctively, or intuitively, knew.

'Who do you think you are?'

I was the elected leader of a remote community.

'Are you afraid of where you are?'

'No.' I was both perfectly calm and at peace with myself. I was merely making one of my regular and routine visits to see that the mausoleum, if that's what it was, was in good order. I always did this alone. The mausoleum, or temple, was some distance from the community's 'city', but still I always went unaccompanied and on foot.

Following the book's instructions, Joy asked, 'What do you wear on your feet? Can you *see* your feet?'

I could indeed. Already I had turned, satisfied that the temple-cum-mausoleum was in perfect order, and I was approaching the open door again. Brilliant sunshine outside almost blinded me. As before, some of it fell through the doorway and to the grooved stone floor and, as I approached, it fell also on to my lower legs and feet.

'Can you *see* your feet?' Joy prompted again.

'Yes.'

'What do you have on them?'

'Nothing.'

'Nothing?'

'My feet are bare.'

'You can see them quite clearly?'

'Vividly.'

'What are they like?'

I did not hesitate, and I was not at all perturbed.

'They are black,' I told them. 'My feet are black.'

I could see this quite clearly—as clearly as I normally see my own *white* feet in actuality. I had exaggerated a little; they weren't exactly black, not as black as a Negro's or a Tamil's, say. They were more coffee-coloured. But coloured they most definitely were. I could see the pink of my toenails and also the pink of the edges of my soles and toes. The toes were very long and rather splayed, used to being bare, and coated with fine dust. There were coarse black hairs on my lower legs, and the legs themselves were very thin and very long.

'I am nearly seven feet tall,' I said.

What was I wearing? A kind of loose robe with holes for the

neck and arms, knee-length, embroidered with brocade at the hem and on all edges, about three inches wide. The material was of a coarsely woven yet lightweight and soft-feeling kind of hessian. I wore nothing underneath.

'What do you have on your head?'

Nothing. At least, no hat or cap. But there was a band of the same brocade round my head. Above the band, my head was long and attentuated and covered with thick, coarse, curly black hair, fairly short-cropped. On the third finger of my right hand—brown-skinned, pink on the palms and under the finger-nails—I wore a very large golden ring with the largest blue stone, probably a sapphire, I had ever seen. In my ears I wore elaborately carved ivory ear-rings inserted through pierced lobes. In my nose I wore very small carved ivory ornaments, as large as modestly-sized buttons or cuff-links. These were linked together and my nose was pierced between the nostrils to hold them. These ornaments—ring, ear-rings, nose-pieces—were, like the brocaded band round my head, insignia of my position or office. I was perfectly accustomed to wearing them without any discomfort whatsoever, and knew that I had been used to them for a good many years.

I was thin and tall, but my weight and size were normal for my kind. I could see my face quite clearly. It too was long and thin, but with finely chiselled features. The lips and eyes were very large, the nose long and narrow. It was both very different from my own 'present' face and yet at the same time still bore some resemblance to it.

I was *inside* that body and I could feel it move, and feel it 'feeling' the cold inside the mausoleum and the heat of the sun outside, just exactly as I could with my own, or present, body.

But now I was outside again. I was standing just outside the mausoleum with its huge rough-hewn walls looming up behind me. Before me the earth spread wide and flat, falling away gradually in a great expanse of near-desert that was almost blinding in the sun. And just as blinding was the narrow yet deep, dark blue, almost black river flowing, with only slight curves here and there, to the far horizon and becoming lost in the haze of heat and dust. Here and there throughout this immense landscape before me were small oases with, from this distance, toy-like fronds that were palms. Nearer, but still below me, was a 'city'.

It was *my* city. I was its elected leader. This was perfectly clear to me. I had not 'inherited' it, through any family lineage of kings or chieftains; I had been elected, as was the custom. But I was *not* one of them—I came from different stock. My 'people' were much smaller in stature, and darker in skin, than I. When I died, and was buried in my sarcophagus in the mausoleum behind me, another would be elected to take my place. And this would always be so. I did not have to be told this; I knew.

My city was a conglomeration of small, white, circular, dome-roofed, stone and mud huts clustered together so that only pedestrians could pass between, even if there had been vehicles of any kind (which there weren't). In the centre of the city was one taller building, only about twice the height of all the rest; this was my 'palace'. It was bright and clean, but spare and simple in line and design. If anything it was almost austere. And now I was walking back to it.

I walked through the 'streets' no wider than paths between the houses of my subjects who, at that time of day, were working in irrigated fields. Women and children hid themselves, as was the custom decreed by the law of the community, for only fully-grown men were permitted to look upon me.

I entered the palace, its large, oval entry-hall cool and bright and pale green all around me. Servants, perhaps half a dozen or so of them, came from outer rooms to bow with folded arms and ask me if I wanted food and water. I didn't and, with a customary gesture of one hand, bade them leave.

I walked the full length of the hall and then turned left through a narrow archway into a small antechamber, brightly lit by sunlight pouring down through a window without glass. In the centre of the room was a stone desk, about the size of an ordinary office desk, plain but beautifully made of rich and gleaming stone or marble.

A backless chair was made of the same material, placed so that the light would fall over my shoulder on to the large stone tablet on which I had been working for several of my twenty-eight or so years. The hieroglyphics were beautifully executed, in precise, neat rows, and brightly coloured.

As I sat down to look through (rather than just *at*) them yet once again, I felt, not despair, but a kind of resigned regret that hieroglyphics served to communicate only the visual and the physical aspects of those things I wished to write about; they completely failed to cope with the abstractions which concerned me so much more. But no other form of written communication had yet been invented. There was no alphabet. I knew that there would be one some day, at some time still in the far-distant future, just as I knew that Jesus Christ had not yet been born. But there would be no way for me in that lifetime, as I was *then*, to communicate any of the many things I wanted to record. I had to content myself with the purely concrete aspects of life—and these were such a small part of my lifetime's experiences, or even of myself as a person, which I craved to recount for posterity. But this would have to wait—*for some other time*.

I was not at all depressed at the thought; it was merely one more thing that I knew I must accept. Sometime, somewhere, a way would be found for man to write of his 'inner' life, his innermost thoughts, of his hopes and fears and aspirations. But this, as yet, was still denied me. I would lead a placid and contented enough life, living to a 'ripe old age' of about thirty-five or so, which was a good lifetime for those days in those parts.

But then a strange thing happened. Having had this revealed to me, my mind, my spirit, my other self, 'overself', call it what you will, suddenly seemed to emerge and float free from the body of my former self, withdrawing to stand in the archway and look back at my former body as it still sat there in the ante-chamber, head supported on clenched hand like Rodin's 'Thinker', and that body in turn still gazing at the hieroglyphic tablet. At the same time I again became aware of being, in actuality, supine on a twentieth-century living-room floor.

'What else can you see?' Joy was saying.

But I was back. The trip, the visitation, whatever it had been, perhaps merely a self-induced or auto-suggested dream, was over. I felt that there was nothing more of it I needed to see or know. Yes, it was over.

Or was it? The whole 'vision' was still perfectly clear in every detail, every shade of colour and nuance of feeling. My companions told me that, for over half an hour, I had recounted and described everything in a voice that had gradually diminished to a quiet monotone. Not only could I remember everything that had 'happened', but now I could answer questions about conditions and circumstances which had not been put to me during the actual time of the 'travelling'. For instance, had I been married? No, I had been single; it had not been permitted for the 'elected one' to marry, which was why he was always elected. I had been 'schooled' in a special place, like a monastery perhaps, from which men like me were elected to rule (or perhaps 'guide' would be more precise) the communities we were sent to.

Of course, I had then spoken a different tongue. It had been a rather ululating language, polysyllabic, a little like the Tamil or Australian aboriginal languages. The time had undoubtedly been long before Christ. The locality had been somewhere in the upper reaches of the Nile. Some day, I knew, the mausoleum would be drowned by an enormous dam that men of the future would build. The Aswan, perhaps? But meanwhile my own time there would be bland and placid. There would be many more elected 'rulers' to follow me; but the community, even the city, would eventually entirely disappear.

About a month has lapsed between the night of the 'experiment' (which, now, I prefer to call an 'experience') and my writing about it now. But all of it, in every detail, is still as vivid as ever it was, much more vivid than any dream and, what is probably a far more salient point, without any of the distortion and unrealistic fantasy of a dream. Whether or not it really was a glimpse of a past life, I am not prepared to say. But at the same time, I am not prepared to dismiss the possibility, just as I cannot yet bring myself either to believe or disbelieve in reincarnation.

But it is an interesting thought, isn't it? And it is certainly a fascinating experience, provided that it is attempted in all seriousness and not with the frivolity of a mere 'party game'. Yet it is certainly more entertaining than any party game—to the extent that I cannot think of anything which has ever absorbed me more. So much so that I found myself wondering whether or not I would ever dare attempt the Christos Experiment again. If I did, would I be shown more of the same 'previous life'? Or would I find myself being transposed—or transmigrated?—into yet another?

More important, perhaps—did the experience fulfil the claim made for it that it solves, or helps one to cope with, a problem in this present life? Well, for about seven years now, my once prolific output in writing has dwindled to almost nothing, due first, to a serious liver disease which left me enervated and lethargic for over three years; and secondly, just as I was recovering, to an injury to my neck that robbed me of over another three years. Oh yes, I admit I *have* managed some sort of output in that time, but only about ten per cent of what it had been before.

I don't yet know whether the visionary revelation in that 'past life', that of finding hieroglyphics a quite inadequate form of communication, will help me now with what is popularly known as 'a writer's block'. All I do know is that, for the first time in many years, I have been able to type this account almost as fast as I could think it. Furthermore, it was written almost entirely in the one sitting. And neither of these things have I been able to do for at least seven years.

Chapter Two

I had thought that this would be the end of it, as should be obvious from the way that first chapter is written. At the time I had no intention of writing more on the matter; indeed, it hadn't even occurred to me. I had written down the experience more for my own satisfaction.

In contrast to what usually happens to most people over very nearly all of their dreams, my memory of the 'journey' did not fade one whit. On the contrary, every detail of it remained fixed in my mind to the extent of my finding myself being reminded of it at least once daily, to begin with, and then two or three times a day. Not only did the details recur to me, but also the colours. And these colours, especially when I had been outside in the sunshine, gazing down on my 'city' and along the winding course of the river to the far horizon, had been as vivid as any I had seen anywhere. Perhaps they had been even more vivid, as sharp as those in Technicolour films or glossy magazines, with the rather overbright colours of picture-postcards. And yet the same also applied to the deep shade to pitch blackness inside the 'mausoleum'. Distances, although far, had seemed, I now recalled, to be rather like those when either viewed through a telescope or photographed through a telescopic lens; but, on the other hand, distortion was not nearly as great as it is in either of these effects. In fact, it had not seemed like distortion at all, but more like being able to see with vastly improved and much more comprehensive eyesight.

The experience, again contrary, perhaps, to what might be expected, did not give me any concern or worry, let alone frighten me. If anything, it seemed to be having the very opposite effect. I felt, somehow, enormously relaxed, relieved about something—perhaps even released. I was considerably calmer about my being able to cope with only a fraction of the amount of work I had been capable of in the past. Not only that; I felt, moreover, that I would now be able to embark on it once more, despite discomfort and frequent pain from my neck and spine injuries which still, after over three years, required regular daily dosages of analgesics.

Could this be the point? All those drugs! At least three of one kind a day, or about 1,000 a year, and six of the other, 2,000 a year—already over 3,000 of one and 6,000 of the other. Were I to accumulate all this into one amount—or even two separate piles of capsules and pills—what an incredible amount it would seem.

I asked my doctor whether any of the possible side-effects from either drug (indocid and norgesic, the latter since exchanged for norflex) would include a predisposition for the facile inducement by some means or other of hallucinations, illusions, or just 'daydreams'. I was assured that no such side-effects had ever been recorded by any of the innumerable patients for whom these drugs were commonly prescribed. Since then I have asked the same thing of several acquaintances in the medical profession—both general practitioners and specialists in very varying fields—and not one has upheld the slightest connection between such an experience and these particular drugs: LSD or opium perhaps, but not of my prescriptions.

At the same time that this journey to another life, in another part of the world and so long ago, kept recurring to me, I also became more and more aware of what the present and 'external' circumstances of my surroundings had been at the time of the 'run'. It had been a winter's evening, but in Western Australia where I was living a winter's evening is very mild indeed compared with those with which I am just as familiar in northern Europe, or northern America for that matter. My hosts had set a wood fire in the room, but it had hardly been chilly enough to light it until, during my 'run', I had proclaimed how cold I had become and had actually started to shiver when I had been inside the mausoleum. Ray, although still sceptical of the whole performance, had then got up and turned on a nearby electric heater. To do so, he had to step over my supine body. I had heard the movement of the radiator, the turning on of the electric fire switch, and had both heard and felt Ray's steps on the carpeted floor near me. In response to some description I had just given (I believe at seeing my own sarcophagus) I also heard him give an involuntary laugh while helping himself to another drink. He had then stepped back over me to return to his own chair on the other side of the room.

This was not the only time he had moved. A little later on he had got up and stepped over me again to turn over the record playing on the radiogram. It was one of the orchestral arrangements of tunes popular in, say, the 'thirties and 'forties, probably played by André Kostelanetz, or someone whose arrangements of music were like his. Certainly it wasn't the kind of 'mood' music which is, I believe, sometimes used at seances and meetings to experiment with the occult—in which, I wish to say here and now, I have never indulged nor been interested in doing so. There was certainly no subduing of lights or lighting of candles and so forth. On the contrary, the room was predominantly white in carpet and furnishings, very modern, and with several lamps turned on, though none of these shone directly into my closed eyes.

Perhaps the strangest sensation, even more than the feeling of having forehead and ankles tending to merge with each other while being massaged, was feeling the warmth of the radiator on my present and *actual* body while simultaneously my past and *adopted* body was experiencing the cold of the mausoleum.

The more I considered the whole thing, the more I came to realize that I was equally aware of both surroundings. Moreover, I had felt convinced that, had I wished, I would have been quite capable of instantly dismissing my 'past life' to return immediately to the present. What's more, I did not think of that present as a greater 'reality' than the past I was visualizing, nor vice versa. Both had been equally real, equally vital, equally personal. And they still are.

One more thing I want to say about the matter as having been recorded at that time: that Joy had been immediately convinced that I had indeed been experiencing all that I had described. But even I was prepared to admit that a woman might be more 'suggestible'. On the other hand, Ray, I knew, had been quite sceptical about the whole matter until very near the end. Then, he told me later, he had the distinctly discomforting conviction that the experience was indeed a reality, and this quite shattered his hitherto very practical and matter-of-fact attitudes, which might be expected from both a construction engineer and an emigrant Norwegian.

I have omitted to record that there was one other person present at the time of this first 'run' of mine—my Dutch friend and assistant, Leo van de Pas, twenty-eight years of age, working with me in Australia on an 'au pair' basis so that he can not only continue his chosen occupation of genealogist but, by retyping my manuscripts and so on, improve his own English to the extent of being able to write in it in the future instead of only in Dutch. He, like Ray, is also a rather practical and down-to-earth person and, perhaps because of the very nature of his chosen occupation, fastidious in detail and veracity. For Leo not even the most convincing verisimilitude, or perhaps veridicality, would be acceptable. But, he told me, he also was quite convinced of the reality of my experience, not only from the expression of my face during the run, the quiet monotone of my voice (which, he said, changed almost completely in character), but more so by the spontaneousness and speed of my description of what I was seeing and experiencing. This, he said, he felt convinced could not be concocted at such short notice even by a novelist used to exerting his imagination to its fullest possible extent. And when he said this at the end of the experiment, Ray agreed with him.

So I suppose I should not have been at all surprised when, a few weeks later, Ray said he wanted to try the experiment himself. I had expected Joy to want to try it, as indeed she did; but she willingly curbed her impatience to allow her husband to try it first; 'If only,' she said, 'because it will be so much more convincing if it succeeds with Ray than if I do it!'

And so it was arranged for the same four of us—Joy and Ray, Leo and I—and only the four of us, to be present at the next experiment with Ray taking the 'trip'.

Chapter Three

It was a little over a month and hence well into the mild winter we have in Western Australia when all four of us again met together at the home of Joy and Ray, this time to take Ray for a 'trip'. The evening was a little cooler than the previous one, and so we had a wood fire burning in the sitting-room section of their extensive living area. Again all lamps were burning, and the radiogram was playing modern music both with and without vocal accompaniment. We had enjoyed a very good dinner with wine to accompany it. It was much like any evening in a suburban home when guests have been invited for dinner. Certainly no preprations had been made to induce a special 'mood'; the only candles which had been lit had been on the dining table some distance away, and these had been extinguished when the meal was over.

There was what could have been regarded as a considerable distraction from the experiment we were about to make, for Joy's two children, a girl of sixteen and a boy of fourteen, were watching a particularly noisy television programme. Although the television room was at the other side of the house, the programme could still be heard distinctly, together with occasional laughter from the children themselves. But once we had started, any distractions seemed almost immediately to become quite negligible.

The relaxing and massaging period of two or three minutes is a pleasant sensation for the person making the trip, though observers can easily become a little impatient to start on the much more interesting part of the procedure. Joy, Ray's wife, had again been elected to 'do the running' while massaging Ray's forehead in a circular motion with the little-finger edge of her cupped hand as before. Meanwhile Leo massaged Ray's

ankles, the latter's shoes having been removed as requ
This left me a completely non-participating observer, whic
particularly wished to be so that I could watch as closely an
carefully as possible all Ray's reactions and expressions during the 'trip'.

In the beginning he seemed to be having more difficulty than I had experienced with the visualizing of first his feet and then his head 'growing' by two, twelve and then twenty-four inches. In each case it took him well over a minute before he could accomplish this visualization. Joy tried first to give him extra encouragement, then to hasten him a little. But Ray wouldn't be hurried. He was taking the procedure quite seriously and, if anything, he became a little annoyed at his wife's impatience, insisting that he should take his own 'good time'. Joy had to curb her impatience until, with each step, Ray had achieved the visualization required of him. But it was soon apparent that he was becoming increasingly proficient at it with each of the steps required of him, although he was not anywhere near as fast at this visualization as I had been.

But if Ray was slower in the visualizing of the stretching or 'growing' exercises, he soon caught up when it came to expanding. No sooner had he been told to imagine himself expanding in all directions than an expression indicating that he suddenly found the procedure pleasingly simple to manage became clearly visible to the three of us, and we hardly had time to look at each other with either a knowing wink or *moue* when Ray told us that he found this part of it so much easier to accomplish. He could, he said, *feel* himself growing, 'enormously', all over, especially in his arms and legs, and even to his toes and fingers. He could not only feel it, he told us, he could also see it happening to him. His body, he said, had become like an enormous balloon. And he was floating. He could, he admitted, still feel his ordinary body lying there on the floor; and feel, too, the pressures of the floor against his back from head to heel. But he could also feel this new and inflated body floating above the floor. And it was all too obvious that he was pleased with himself for achieving this entirely new sensation.

Then Joy started him off on the memory tests. Perhaps as an engineer should, he was very easily able to describe their front door (actually double doors, with heavy mouldings and brass ornaments) in minute detail. And again it was obvious that he found great pleasure in being able to do this. He described the plants, ranging from small annuals to large semi-tropical plants and even a banana tree, which grew in the courtyard in front of the doors, and the glass windows and walls surrounding them. He spent several minutes describing it all and, when we asked him what time of day it was as he visualized it, he answered immediately, 'Daytime, of course.' Then corrected himself with, 'I mean, I know it's night-time now, but it's *day*time while I'm looking at the doors.'

This, of course, immediately fascinated me, for it was part of the procedure which I had inadvertently missed. I had, as you will remember, gone out from my cathedral straight to the door of the mausoleum instead of following this procedure. Leaning forward, I could see the slight frown of effort Ray made when he was instructed to do or describe something, then this frown being erased by an expression of spontaneous pleasure at doing whatever he had been asked to do. And it was also very plain to see that he intended doing everything as thoroughly as it was possible to do it.

Next, he was to imagine he was on the roof of his house and looking around the garden below. To my surprise, he could do this immediately. I had thought it would be necessary for him to be coaxed or guided for a while, but not at all. Before any of us could say anything additional to Joy's instruction, he was 'there'! And he could describe everything, even the plants and shrubs and the considerable layout of both front and back gardens, down to the smallest detail. Not only that, but he could describe the houses next door, on either side, from this rather unusual viewpoint from the top of the roof of his own house. It did occur to me to ask him, knowing how active he was as a handyman around the house, if he had been there in actuality, either recently or at all. He immediately replied that he had been up there, but not for some time, many months in fact, and not since the two houses to the north of his had been built. Yet he could see and describe those houses from this viewpoint as though he was actually up there.

Once more he was asked what time of day it was, and again he immediately replied that it was daytime, probably about mid-afternoon, as everything was so bright and clear. Not only could he see the houses on either side, but also the roads both at the back and in front of the house. It was still daytime, he said, and there were cars parked in the sunlight on the far side of the road in front of the house and there was also quite a lot of traffic—although in actuality it was late at night, with little traffic, and no cars at all parked there. Of all this he was equally aware, he told us, while at the same time seeing it through his closed eyes in such very different circumstances.

Beyond the road lies the sea, the Indian Ocean, with a steep decline to a beautiful beach that, almost from this very point, stretches in a wide and gentle curve to the north, with no visible habitation after a few hundred yards or so. On the horizon lies Rottnest Island, only about three or four miles of it visible from this angle. Ray could describe all of this. What was more, he was still seeing it as though it was a bright summer day and not the wintry night it was in reality. Had he been allowed to do so, he would have gone on giving us details of everything he could see until the evening had gone without any 'journey' being accomplished.

His next instruction was to imagine himself going up five hundred feet into the air directly above the house. This, I thought to myself, would be bound to prove more difficult for him, but I soon found myself very much mistaken. There was indeed a slight frown of effort for a moment, but a very fleeting moment, before he was again exhibiting his pleased expression of having achieved what was required of him.

'Are you *there*?' Joy asked him.

'Yes' was the immediate answer.

He was indeed. As it was still daylight for him, he could see for miles around, and all he saw he could still describe in the minutest detail—it obviously delighted him to do so. Furthermore, we were able to check afterwards on several observations he made which, although all four of us lived in the district and close to the beach, the rest of us had not been aware of until Ray's descriptions made on his living-room floor, at night, and with his eyes firmly closed.

But this description is already imprecise. His eyes were not firmly closed all the time. When he was 'seeing' something for the first time, the closed lids would flicker quite rapidly. Our 'guide-book' said that this denoted that it was the spiritual mind, or 'overself', and not the ordinary conscious mind of the body, which was responsible for depicting what he described.

This experience I had also missed, and from Ray's excited enjoyment of it all, I already regretted that I had.

However, it was equally fascinating and enjoyable to observe each step of the procedure. Now Ray was told to change the scene he was watching from daytime to night-time. It took him only a matter of five to ten seconds and it was done. Then he was told to change it back to daytime again. He could do this with equal facility. But now he was asked who was responsible for this changing of the scene from day to night and back to day again—and he answered without having to think about it that he himself was. Moreover, he himself had complete control of whatever altitude he wanted to take, moving rapidly through the air much as only a Flying Saucer is described as doing. He could change the scene at will from day to night and even, from a height of approximately 30,000 feet, from season to season, describing the sea and sky with wintry storms at one stage, then summer glare, then with the rich colours of autumn sunsets, and even with the sea calm and scintillating in moonlight.

He had travelled so high that he could clearly see all of the city some eight miles away, the curves and bays of the Swan River estuary approaching and circumscribing it, the hills of the Darling Ranges some twenty miles to both north and south, and out over the sea and even over the island of Rottnest, about eleven miles away, as though looking down on it. Then he went even higher—so high that houses and then the grid-pattern of the suburbs became indistinct. He could distinguish, he said, little more than land, sea and sky. We looked at each other, knowing he was now ready to be 'brought down to earth' and 'another life'.

Almost immediately, he told us, it became late afternoon and evening again, no matter how much he was exhorted to keep the time to noon of a sunny day. His forehead would wrinkle, but after a while he could merely say no, he couldn't keep it to daylight, but that it didn't matter because he was already down to earth again and safely on land. And he could hardly wait to describe it.

He was coming on to the land from water. It was hard for him to see, he said, as it was growing dark. The water was calm but very dark, almost black. No, it wasn't the ocean as he, and we three, had expected. It was a lake—a lake surrounded by mountains. He worked with boats on the lake, and he had come to the shore and the village where he lived. He couldn't see what he was wearing in the way of clothes, some kind of heavy crude boots, he thought, and some kind of rough clothing he couldn't define. Yet he knew and could see his own long, blond, wavy hair falling down past his shoulders, and a long blond beard that hid almost all of his face. His hands, he said, were enormous. He worked with his hands and they were very hard and strong. In real life he worked by day as one of the senior engineers in the office of a large engineering company. Any manual labour he did was performed at home; and though he did indeed do a fair amount of work round house and garden, he made a point of telling us that his hands, then, were much bigger and stronger and harder than his hands of the present. Indeed, he said, his whole body was bigger and stronger.

He was approaching the village from a rough kind of jetty, a rather small and crude construction. The village was composed almost entirely of small timber huts. He thought the roofs were thatched. There were doorways, but no doors; window-openings but no glass panes or shutters. The village nestled between tall dark trees with the mountains rising abruptly behind and it had, he thought, about twenty or thirty of these wooden huts. Yes, there were other people there, but he couldn't see them. He couldn't see anyone. But he did know that there were people there, people dancing and singing somewhere a little way off from the village. He himself had been working late, and in any case he was alone. What was more, he was aware of being a very lonely person. He had no one—no family, no parents, no wife or children.

Then he went inside one of the huts. There was a fire burning, but the flames were very low. Apart from the fire, it was very dark inside the hut, almost black, now that the evening was drawing on into nightfall. The only bright thing he could see anywhere was the fire's small flames and glowing coals. He had to wait for his eyes to become accustomed to the gloom.

After a short while, he said he could now make out a rough table. And on the table was a crude ceramic bowl containing water. Hanging on pegs around the walls of the hut were rough mugs to use for dipping into the bowl for drinking water.

As there were several mugs, he now knew that the hut was used by several people, though at the time he was the only one there.

What part of the world did he think he was in? In Norway, his native land. But no, not where he had been born and brought up—nowhere at all near Oslo—he was somewhere high up in the mountains, in a small village on the bleak shore of a mountain lake. The water was very deep, which was why it was so very dark, almost black.

Had he been there before? No, never. But he had seen country like it, in both Norway and Sweden, possibly also in Finland.

He was very definitely back in his own part of the world? Yes, he had no doubt of it.

Did he like being there? No. No? No, it was cold—much too cold. He wanted to live somewhere where the climate was warmer. Instead of having just a mountain lake, he wanted to go to sea, then sail to a land where it was always warm. Here he was always cold. And it seemed almost always to be dark. And always he was alone.

'You're not married?'

'No.'

'Do you have any family? Father, mother—brothers or sisters?'

'No one.'

'Girl friend?'

'No. And that's what I want. A wife, children.'

'Is there nobody there suitable for you?'

'No. I have to leave this place and look somewhere else for a wife.'

'You said there were people there, singing and dancing?'

'Yes.'

'Can you see any of them now?'

He obviously tried, for he frowned with the effort and his eyes again flickered rapidly.

'No, I can't see them. They are somewhere just beyond the village.'

'What time of day is it?'

'It's night-time now. It's very dark.'

'You remember that you previously changed day into night, and then night into day?'

'Yes.'

'Can you do it again, then? Now?'

And again it was quite perceptible that he was trying. His hands clenched, two fingers of one hand making the motion of tapping a table, but without touching the floor. They merely tapped the air just above the floor. Then they became still. His hands relaxed and came to rest once more on the floor beside his thighs.

'You can't do it?'

'No.'

'But you could before?'

'That was different. That was just an exercise. This—'

And then he made the most incredible statement of the evening.

'This is—*real*.'

But he was, now, also awake—or *back*—whichever way you want to regard it. His eyes opened. He looked round him and then sat up. He was not at all disturbed at being back in a twentieth-century living-room—in his own home—with the three of us again. In fact, when I asked him, he had, like myself, been aware of these *actual* surroundings—and of us—all the time. What was more, he now needed to move away from the fire, rubbing the thigh which had been a little too near to it with a rather rueful smile. But then, even as he did so, the rueful smile gave way to an expression of perplexity.

'It's funny,' he said, 'but although I'm warm from the fire here, I remember that I was cold, terribly cold, even on the same leg, when I was—*there*.'

'Do you really feel that you've been back to a previous life, Ray?'

He didn't even hesitate.

'Oh, no doubt about it! Unless it was—well, you know—like a dream. But it was too real for that. It was as real as being here right now.'

'How long ago do you think it was?'

'Oh, long ago!' And again there had been no hesitation, and no doubt whatsoever.

'Hundreds of years?'

'Hundreds? Thousands! I'd say at least eight, nine, maybe ten thousand years ago.'

'As long as that!'

'Oh, yes.'
'How can you tell?'
'Well, everything was so—primitive.'
'But there are still primitive places like you described existing today.'
'We were also so primitive. I was.'
'Were you still an engineer?'
'Lord, no! There wasn't any such thing then.'
'What did you do, then—for a living?'
'Worked on boats. Something to do with boats.'
'And you really think it all happened?'
'It happened just then, all right.'
'No, that's not what I meant. What I mean is—you really feel as though what you saw had all happened to you once before, a long time ago?'
And again there was no hesitation.
'Oh, yes,' he said.
'Would you swear to it?'
'I would.'
'Doesn't it surprise you?'
'It shatters me,' he replied. 'But it's all true just the same. In fact, I—'
'Yes?'
'Well, I came out of it so quickly, I'd—rather like to try it again.'

We were all convinced by then that at least he had, as I had before him, experienced something which had not only been tremendously real to him, but was something he, again like me, had never experienced before. It had all been too vivid and too logical and too real to be a dream or any kind of hallucination. He most certainly could not have concocted it all, just as I myself, novelist or not, could not have concocted my own experience. And his wife, Joy, assured us that Ray would never treat a matter like this lightly, let alone with levity or playful duplicity.

However, there were still two possible explanations that occurred to me, at least so far as Ray's experience was concerned. First of all, none of us had experienced a 'trip' induced by drugs, whether by LSD, or Aldous Huxley's Mexican drug, mescalin, or the milder marijuana; so we could not tell whether this experience, induced by a little massage and mental exercise, was similar. Secondly, it could be a kind of 'illustration' of an old wish, a yearning, from Ray's early childhood—and of course I mean his present childhood. He had always wanted to leave the cold and long northern winters of his native Norway and, as a young man, had migrated first to the United States, just after the Second World War, and then here to Western Australia some fifteen years ago. So it could, then, have been a kind of mental depiction of his urge to escape the cold of Scandinavia.

There was also one other matter which rather disappointed me. His experience had been so much shorter than mine, and depicted in such gloom. But when I pointed this out, he protested that although the evening itself had been dark, and the interior of the hut so gloomy that he could see little colour except the flames and coals of the fire, nevertheless he had seen everything with an incredible clarity and sharpness, as though he was seeing things—particularly the texture of the walls and drinking bowl—through a telescope, or magnifying glass. Despite the darkness of his vision, his sight had still had the same incredible intensity as my own.

Was he at all disturbed by the experience?

'No, not at all. I think it was marvellous. It makes you feel so—so, well, relaxed. Calmer about things. As though I've been relieved of something that has been troubling me—worrying me even.'

And this, too, was exactly how I myself still felt about my own experience. It was an even further relief to have someone else, and especially someone as logical and practical as Ray, share this experience and attitude towards it.

Finally, 'I definitely want to try it again,' he said.

Chapter Four

But of course, no one was going to have a second run before Joy and then Leo had had their first. Again we left it for two or three weeks before taking another run. Not only was the time factor involved—for each trip usually took about an hour, including the preparations; then discussion afterwards took almost as long again—but there was a feeling of something between exhaustion and a calm satisfaction experienced by the observers as well as the person being run. By this time it was well into winter, or about mid-June in the Antipodes, when it was Joy's turn. I was to run her with Ray massaging her ankles.

As we had expected, she went through the preliminary exercises after massage quite easily, finding little trouble in growing at either end or in expanding, despite three men joking at the time, and quite audibly, that this would be the last thing a woman would want to do, let alone admit to doing. She did seem to have a little more difficulty in describing the front doors of their house, even though Ray had described them with such facility previously. When this happened, it occurred to me that perhaps men were better at remembering details than women; but she was soon able to show that she was as proficient as Ray and I are at memorizing, or visualizing, once she was on the roof looking down and around her. And when she 'went up into the air', she soon started to complain of the cold even though she was lying within a few feet of a rather warm fire. When she guessed her altitude (from aeroplane flights) to be around 30,000 feet, she began to shiver quite violently. I was about to fetch a rug to cover her when she began 'to come down' again. Her shivering eased. When she had 'landed', it stopped altogether. She was again perfectly relaxed. After a moment or so, there was the familiar frown and flickering eyelids. Then one hand rose and began to waver around.

This time Leo had thought to bring a tape-recorder, which he now switched on. This is the true conversation with myself as 'runner', transcribed verbatim from the tape.

J. I've landed.

G. Safely? On the ground?

J. Yes.

G. Can you see your feet?

J. Yes. And my hands. I have *beautiful* hands! My nails are all painted. They've got birds painted on them!

G. Birds?

J. Little birds! Little beautiful birds!

G. What are you wearing? Shoes? Stockings?

J. I have beautiful hands! Very beautiful hands! And my toenails are painted, too.

G. What colour are they?

J. Blue. Green-blue. Like, like—

G. In patterns?

J. —Like—like opals!

G. Like opals?

J. Like beautiful enamels.

G. No patterns? No birds?

J. Bird? On my right hand, and on my left hand—tiny jars.

G. Tiny jars?

J. Tiny jars. Beautiful little, delicate jars. The fingers of my hands are beautiful. They *are* beautiful!

G. What are you wearing?

J. I'm very dainty. I'm very tiny, but I am a woman.

G. You are a woman. Do you have a name?

J. I have a long neck—a very long neck.

G. A very long neck; but you are tiny?

J. I wouldn't be five feet tall.

G. What colour hair do you have? Can you see your hair? Is it long hair or short hair? You can't see you hair?

J. It is reddish-brown. (In actuality it is blonde.)

G. Is it long or short hair?

J. Long, but very fine. And plaited in many plaits. They are hanging from my temples.

G. Is there anything *in* your hair?

J. I have a blue ribbon in my hair.

G. Of what sort of material is it?

J. It is metal. And it's got lots of turquoise, and blue, and mauve and purple, and it's fine and it's around my head. And my reddish-brown hair comes down. I'm *very* tiny!

G. And what do you wear?

J. I have a white garment on me. A simple white garment.

G. Does it have sleeves?

J. No sleeves. I can describe it in perfect detail, it is so clear. A fine white linen garment, and I am wearing nothing underneath it. It is held by a soft cord, and it is down to my calves.

G. Is there a lot of material?

J. No, it seems to have some pleating, or folds. I seem to be very preoccupied with my appearance. My hands are beautiful! They are exquisite!

G. Is there very much make-up on your face?

J. None at all. I seem to have—like absolute alabaster skin. Like the blood is drained from me. I have a very strange feeling within me.

G. And is it warm where you are? Can you see what is just around you? Are you in a street, or a square, or in a house or garden? Can you see where you are?

J. I am on white marble steps. I seem to be there already, but I don't know how I got there. I am against the steps and there are two white pillars on either side, and they are long white pillars.

G. And is there just the one step?

J. There are about eight, and I am on the middle one.

G. And are you looking down?

J. I am looking down and there is reddish-brown sand and oasis trees. And it is a hot afternoon and I am coming down the steps.

G. Can you feel the hot sand under your feet when you are coming down?

J. No, I am still on the steps, and they are cool.

G. The marble feels cool?

J. I seem to be very disturbed.

G. Are you alone?

J. I am by myself, but I'm very upset. I don't know what the feeling is. I'm bewildered. I'm lost, I think.

G. And there is nobody around you?

J. I am coming towards a building. It seems to be on my right. A long, narrow, *red* building. And it's got colonnades, with white pillars. About twelve pillars. Hard earth beneath there, and little doorways. There are women and children sitting on rough benches. And I am walking towards them.

G. Are there many women and children?

J. Several, and they don't take much notice of me.

G. Can you see what they look like, and what they are dressed in?

J. Their faces are hanging, like they are sad. Like they are crying.

G. The children too?

J. Mostly the children. It seems as though they have lost something—something special—I am walking towards them.

G. How old do you think you are as you walk towards them?

J. About twenty-four. Not more. I am very beautiful.

G. Are you married?

J. I don't know. I seem to be something symbolic to these people. I don't know what I am, but I am terribly pre-occupied by the beauty of my body, and the exquisite proportions of those beautiful hands. They are *so* exquisite! My long, thin neck! My face has a very fine bone structure, and a very big mouth.

G. Do you know what your name is?

J. Minna comes to me. Minna.

G. Do you have brothers and sisters? Any near one? Any other family?

J. I have got a father. He is a type of ruler. He has very grey hair...I have just decided to walk back from that building and I am going back up the steps into this building with the high pillars. He is sitting down there, and he's got his head in his hands, and he is also in a sad spirit. He has sandals on his feet. He is a man of about fifty, grey hair and fine temples, and *very* bronze. Brown skin; reddish-brown skin. He is also finely built, like me, and he has got grey eyes. Beautiful blue-grey eyes. And a fine nose. He's got a golden cord around his head. And he seems to be worried. He's got his head in his hands and he is thinking. No, he is also sad. Everybody is sad.

G. Do you feel sad yourself?

J. I feel—I am *out* of myself, and I don't think I'm really there.

G. Can you see any details?

J. Do you know what? I am *dead*! And they are all crying *because* I am dead. That's why I am so agitated in myself. My body within me—that's why I am so preoccupied with my body. I am looking at it, and I know I am dead!

G. But your body is able to move?

J. And I am moving about like I am alive! But I know I am dead! They all seem to be sorry. They are *all* sad.

G. Do you know how you died? Do you know how long ago it is?

J. I died with a pain in my head. I died only that morning. And I am walking round all the places I used to know.

G. You think you are looking at them for the last time?

J. I seem to go around bewildered, because nobody sees me. Nobody recognizes me. I'm not seen by *any* of them. Nobody sees me at all. I'm walking around, that's why I am lost.

G. Can you see anybody else that they *cannot* see?

J. They are all crying their eyes out.

G. You can't see anybody who has died before you?

J. No. It is as if I am completely cut off. I am walking around in this stone courtyard now. A stone courtyard. It is as clear as anything. And he is sitting down on a stone chair and he is crying. There are a few pillars behind him, and there is an archway and there is lots of sunlight. And there are cats walking about in the garden.

G. What colour cats? Are they all colours? Or white cats or black cats?

J. There are white cats—and a white and grey cat. They are long lean cats—My father looks up at me, and around and up at the sunlight. He is terribly sad. I go to speak to him and he doesn't hear me...And there is a little boy sitting next to him. He must be about three years of age. He is my brother. And he is tugging at my father's arm and asking him why, why is he crying. And my father says because your sister died today.

G. And do you have a mother still?

J. I don't know.

G. Do you know whereabouts you are in the world?

J. Somewhere in Italy. In Rome. I *feel Roman*...I go up the white steps. I've left them; I've given them away. (Her father, brother and mourners.) I am going up the steps. I am walking into a huge, arched door; and there is a beautiful vault at each side in red and gold and black. And there is some kind of corridor. I'm turning right and I'm going up further beautiful marble steps. And they have got long pillars. I am going to my room.

G. Are you going into your room?

J. Yes, I am walking into my room.

G. What do you see in your room?

J. It is a beautiful room. And I am lying on a table. My—body—! I am standing by the door—and I am *looking at my body*!

G. You can *see* your own *body*?

J. And I am dressed exactly as I stand.

G. You are no longer in that body now?

J. No—and I am standing there looking at it. And I am very peaceful-looking. And my eyes are closed, on the table, and my hands are crossed on my breast and I am holding some gold—gold—metal bar, with blue stones in it. It has been put in my hands as they crossed them over my chest.

But I am so tiny!...

And I am looking at my body, and that's why I am so white. I've got no blood left in me. An absolute alabaster white.

G. You are looking down on it?

J. I am standing by, at the head of my body, and I am looking down on it. And a *won*derful feeling comes to me—this is really what happens when you die. There is nothing to be frightened of—nothing. It is all a myth.

And that's what's running through my mind now.

But I know I am not real. I feel you could put air right through me. It is a fantastic sensation. And all I am looking at is a beautiful—statue, and stone, with carvings ahead. And this room is beautiful. There is sunlight coming in from everywhere. And the dome of the ceiling is red and gold, in a magnificent design. Polished floors. Marble floors. And the colours are grey—very distinctly, metal-grey—with beautiful white insets. And this beautiful rusty-red in the shapes of large curves...

There is a lot of gilt! *Lots* of gilt!...

I am quite happy now, having seen my body. I know I'm dead. And what really delights me, really *pleases* me, is that this thing that everybody is frightened of is death. And it's like *walking into a room*! It's just like *walking* into *another room*!...

I wonder what they'll do with me!

But the funny, strange feeling is that I am standing there looking at my body, and it was very beautiful. And it doesn't seem to worry me what they do with it, because to me it doesn't matter any more...

I feel very skittish now. Before I was bewildered, but now I feel like I—I'd like to sit around and play a trick with myself, and see what they'll do with me. But something tells me I shouldn't do that, because that wouldn't be nice! That wouldn't be respectful!...

G. You still see yourself outside that body?

J. Yes. It is so *clear*, it is marvellous. It is the most wonderful experience, to have had this. I am dead and there is no question about it. And it isn't worrying me one bit.

G. Can you see anything more of your father?

J. He doesn't seem to be there. It doesn't seem to matter about him any more.

G. Now you know he is not with you, can you remember what his name was?

J. No. But he was a man of royalty, and I was either a princess or something. But I am very important because the whole city is sad. Everybody is sad I am dead and I am so young. And I am so beautiful, and I am dead.

G. Did you never marry?

J. Never married.

G. Have you been in love at all?

J. Never been in love. That is why they feel—so sad. I was considered skittish, frivolous, but sweet to everybody. Frivolous, like a pet! Like a sweet pet, they thought I was. A sweet pet...

Everyone is talking about me now, and I can hear them say I was a sweet pet, a sweet pet...

G. And your family was rich?

J. Very rich.

G. You were spoiled?

J. Oh, *utterly* spoiled! It was as if I was a beautiful, grown-up child.

G. Did you do anything?

J. Nothing.

G. Do your remember your life? You didn't dance, paint, or make beautiful things?

J. I am enjoying this so much, you know. It is an incredible experience, to know you are dead and looking at your sarcophagus, and you're not even worried about it. And I am quite convinced this is the way it really is, as I *know* it is. I am very pleased. I was very delicate, and the doctors said that I died of something in my head, a *disease* in my head, or *something* to my head.

G. And did you ever try to do any kind of—anything to pass the time away?

J. Yes. I played the harp. I played a little harp. Just adequately. Not terribly well.

G. Did you ever *want* to do anything?

J. I didn't seem to want to do much. I was utterly spoiled.

G. Did you enjoy your life?

J. Every minute. I loved animals, lots of animals about me. Many cats and dogs. And there is the glorious garden, absolutely exquisite...

And now I can see where I am, it is clear, I am right on the heights of Rome. I am looking right over Rome. It is unbelievable! It is misty and pink and mauve, and I must be very high up on the height of a high mountain. And I am somewhere in Rome. Somewhere on the heights of Rome. And it is just a little before Christ. Christ hasn't been to Italy. A very pagan life I led.

G. Did you worship pagan gods?

J. I did it because I—it was considered right for me to. It didn't worry me. I was very frivolous. *Very* frivolous! And very beautiful...

But I know where I am; I am right on the heights of Rome. I am looking down into the old city. The distance—incredible! I can see all the Tiber, trees.

G. While you look down all over this distance, and you are no longer in the body of the girl you saw, can you now feel yourself lying on the floor here? Can you do both at once?

J. I *am* doing that! This is the fantastic thing! I don't want to leave, there is so much excitement here for me. I am lying on the floor but I am also walking around in the temple, in a sort of strange sense. And I know where I am, and I see all the colours and the beauty of where I belong. And yet I know I am dead. And something is telling me I am not allowed to stay here very long, because I am dead. I am just told that I must leave this, to go elsewhere. But I don't want to leave. I want to stay, because it is a beautiful day and the sunlight is pouring in...

It's Rome, it's Italy, in the early centuries. The trees, the buildings! The beautiful mist rising up from the sea! The heights!...

G. But you can still feel yourself also back on the floor here?

J. Yes, I feel very agitated and tied up in a knot on the floor. But I feel very free away from it. It is a fantastic feeling.

G. You can see everything very clearly? Clearer than in a dream?

J. Oh, *much* sharper!

G. Is it as clear as, say, when you are looking at a film?

J. As perfect as that! As perfect!

I can go into incredible detail without even thinking of it...

I seem to be away from the temple I was in.

I've left that! I *must* have—I've left it...

G. You know where you are?

J. I am leaving, and I am up in the air. I am going many thousands of feet up in the air—and the city is fading from me. I know I've *got* to leave. My body is gone and I can't look back. I don't want to look back. I'm *frightened* to look back. And I'm going out over the sea again. I'm up high over the sea again and I'm getting terribly tired in my body on the floor. My body is very agitated. *Very* exhausted.

G. And you are back here now?

J. It's gone black! All black!

G. You are back here now?

J. Ooh! (She opened her eyes.)

G. It's unbelievable, isn't it!

J. Ooh! What an experience! It's frightening, but it's marvellous! It could explain why I always get my headaches!

But I was the most beautiful, beautiful thing!

G. You can see it, can't you.

J. *Clearly*! I will give you an exact drawing of me! But my hands were that *beau*tiful! And tiny! I had a similar body that I have now. Tiny wrists. Slight and tiny.

But my skin was absolutely alabaster. You know when I first—I can remember everything—when I first said my skin is absolutely parchment white? Like it had no blood in it at all?

G. Yes.

J. Drained of every—this was the thing that shocked me,

when I looked down at my feet, at my little feet—and the toenails were painted, a beautiful—like white enamel! Each toenail. And it was this beautiful bird's wing, with a beak. And on the little toes I had jars. Little jars. Little red ochre jars were superimposed on the nail.

G. You must have seen it so clearly, because you described it so well.

J. Oh! It left me absolutely ga-ga!

G. When I came back I too was amazed at how vivid it all was.

J. You know, I was terribly cold when I jumped 30,000 feet. I automatically *soared* up to 30,000 feet! I knew it was 30,000 feet from the time I had been in an aircraft. The distance you *then* see, you *know*...

I looked down, and the body wanted to *go* to the spot it ultimately landed on. I was impatient to go to this coastline. I landed on this reddish—pinkish-reddish was the word—pinky-red sand. Now this is Roman sand, isn't it? Pinky-red?

G. I think it is.

J. It is a pinky-red. Sort of dirty reddish-pink. And it wasn't like our white sand...

I don't know what I was, but I was very important in the community. I was symbolic to the community...You know, when I landed on this reddish-brown land, and I saw this sort of funny building, suddenly I knew there were steps behind me, and that they were marble. And I felt the big building at the back of me. But I didn't *look* back, because I knew if I looked back there wouldn't be any more for me. That was the feeling I had. I was still on the steps when I described myself, and I was absolutely taken up by that body of mine! The *white*ness of the body! And I suddenly felt the body was looking outside myself, and thinking it is not real. And as I walked into that direction there were three palm trees there, and there were these women sitting down wailing. Lots of women, sitting by the colonnade. Sitting like away from the main building, and they were sitting there obviously weeping. And when I seemed to walk up past them and said, 'Look I am here, what's wrong with you!' they didn't see me. They *just didn't see me*...

I think the recorded words here speak for themselves without need for much comment. But I do want to point out that here, for the first time, something slightly approaching the sinister appeared. I am not referring to Joy's rather amazing and perhaps very comforting vision of death, but to her comment that she had died in *that* life of something, a tumour perhaps, wrong with her head. For in this life (and you will note that unconsciously I have already started referring to 'that' and 'this' life) she has suffered from migraine headaches for a number of years, headaches which give her such pain and make her physically so ill that she must frequently take to her bed for hours, sometimes days.

You may be surprised that I myself have expressed no dismay at the very convincing *experience* of death she had described, of her being in a 'spiritual state' yet with the same physical, if perhaps ghostlike, appearance as her own body lying before her in death, and more especially of death being 'just like walking into another room'. It would take too long for me to recount all the years I spent in Singapore and in Malaya, but it was then that I heard very much the same thing from Indian and consequently rather mystic friends. Some Chinese, mostly of an older generation, had also confided their beliefs about death, and they were very much like Joy's description. This seems fairly common as an Asian belief, or acceptance, of what death is. It might give the Western world a great deal of comfort in our attitudes towards life if we could adopt a similar view, instead of the prevalent abhorrence and fear that most of us have of death.

I was not at all surprised by Joy's description, but I was surprised, as I think all three of us were, that her first glimpse of what we had been led to believe should be a former life had turned out to be a former death. Then there was the other 'purpose' of these revelations to consider—that we are given an experience relevant to a problem in present life.

If this were so, did it mean that Joy might die from the same complaint, considering how much she suffers from migraine in this present life of hers? In my case, it was quite obvious that had there been any pertinent point or 'message' to my own revelation, it was that I had only to consider the limitations of hieroglyphics in communicating one's thoughts for me to overcome my writer's block and be more than content with my lot of writing—writing almost anything at all, I had come to a persistent sense of the futility of even a 'great' novel, a waste of precious time compared with just the living of life itself. And with Ray I think it was perfectly obvious that he had previously longed to leave the dark and cold of Scandinavian winters for a warmer and brighter climate. This indicated that he should, perhaps, overcome a certain amount of restlessness which assailed him quite frequently here in Australia, despite both his accomplishments in his work and the acquisition of a home he feels sure would have been denied him had he remained in his native Norway, and that he should be content with his lot where he had chosen to live.

But Joy herself did not see anything sinister at all in the death aspect. For weeks she was enthralled and fascinated by the experience. She thought that if there was any point to her revelation then it was that she had wasted one life with frivolity and 'kittenishness', very considerable traits in her present character, though a part, too, of her just-as-considerable charm. Another point was that she has always adored and strived to surround herself with beautiful things—and not only herself but others as well, by working for a number of years as an interior decorator. She felt convinced that her character then was much as it was now. She also felt, she told us, that, contrary to her preference and perhaps even hopes, she would always have been a woman and never the man she often proclaimed she would like to be. In the same way (provided, of course, that there was some foundation for belief in past lives and 'incarnations') a man would always have been, and always would be, a man. This seemed to concern her far more than the possibility of her headaches again being the cause of her death, or departure from the 'present' life, as she had already started to refer to it.

There is one more point before I go on to Leo's run, and this is that long before any of us had even heard of the Christos Experiment, we had often conjectured what we might have been had there been such things as previous lives. Joy had frequently proclaimed that she would have been either Egyptian, and looking rather like Queen Nefertiti, or a gypsy. She had been quite convinced of this, she told me, so much so that it gave her a shock to find that in the 'life' just revealed to her she had been nothing of the kind. Similarly, Ray had often said that he would have been a Viking; he used often to jest that he can automatically handle a cutlass as adeptly as any Viking buccaneer! He even confessed that, if any past life had been revealed by this experiment at all, he had expected it to have been that of a pirate. For the sea, he says, has always been in his blood. I think his dark and brooding mountain lake had considerably disappointed him. As for me, I suppose I had expected always to have been a man; I couldn't even visualize myself in the body or role of a woman. But one thing which would never have occurred to me either was that, if there was any possibility at all of having had a past life or even lives, I could be other than European, and my skin other than white. And yet, when this *had* occurred in my own revelation, and I had found myself both coloured and so very different from my present physical appearance, I had not been at all dismayed by it.

Chapter Five

According to the magazine which had introduced this whole matter to me in the first place, 'There must be a deep inner need in the person to find out about their past life experiences *in order to help them cope with this present incarnation.*' (The emphasis was in the magazine.)

I think there must be at least something of that need for the experience to occur at all. I also think that if a person is in the least frightened of it, it simply will not succeed. I believe this applied to the last of our quartet to try the experiment, for with Leo it failed. I will not, however, say that it failed completely, and neither does he. He did indeed experience a kind of 'travelling', but he did not attain even a glimpse of some possibly previous life. On the contrary, he remained very much in the present—except that he happened to be almost exactly on the opposite point of the earth, back in his native Netherlands and, more specifically, in the small town of De Bilt where he was born and brought up, just two or three kilometres from the city of Utrecht.

I suppose we should not have persisted. All through the evening, when we were again at Joy and Ray's home, he had seemed a little quieter than usual, perhaps even apprehensive. And when the time came to start the experiment he suddenly became reluctant. However, possibly because of Joy's expressed disappointment, he allowed himself to be prepared for the experiment after all, with Joy massaging his ankles and I his forehead, since it had been decided that I should take him for his 'trip'.

After several minutes of massaging, we asked him if he was ready. He did seem relaxed enough, until I noticed the tense way he was gripping his hands. At first he said he thought he *was* ready, but then almost immediately he turned to me and, opening his eyes, said he felt that the experiment wouldn't work with him. We, of course, exhorted him at least to try, and so he did. It occurred to me that not so many years ago, when he had been just twenty (at the time of writing he is almost twenty-nine), he had been not at all alarmed, when drafted into the Dutch Army, to be sent to New Guinea. And later, when he was twenty-five, he had taken the risk of journeying from his native Netherlands all the way to Western Australia to work in a low-paid 'au pair' arrangement with me, in order to be able to continue with his chosen vocation of genealogy. Since his arrival here, he had neither expressed nor displayed alarm at the journeys of varying lengths and distances which we made together. Nothing very much ever does seem to alarm Leo, not even the matter of not earning enough to pay his return fare to the Netherlands should something happen to me without my having made adequate provision for him, a situation which I am quite sure would have caused a great deal of anxiety in most other people, even to the extent of their demurring from such a journey to Australia altogether. Because of these things, I fear I did not see that he was genuinely apprehensive of our experiment.

When he did seem relaxed, I, of course, began by giving him the 'stretching' exercises, but from the beginning it was plain that he was having little success. Yet I still didn't suspect that something might be wrong, as Ray had also had his difficulties at the start. It took Leo longer than the stipulated minute, indeed more than two and sometimes three, before he would very softly say a 'Yes', which, as I should have realized at the time, was considerably less than half-hearted. I think (and he confirmed this afterwards) that he found the line of least resistance was to say a grudging 'Yes' when in actual fact he was unable to feel, let alone visualize, this business of stretching at all. And expanding was quite beyond him.

And yet, as I have already said, the experiment with him *wasn't* a complete failure. In fact, far from it. Although he didn't manage to travel to any past life, he did manage to travel the no mean distance of several thousand miles to his native Netherlands on the other side of the earth.

I think the first memory exercises were responsible for this, for when I asked him to visualize his own front door I had of course meant the front door of my apartment, where he now lives. He, however, chose the door of his home in De Bilt. And when I realized that this was in fact what he was describing—and in very full detail at that—I did not bother to interrupt him and have him start again. In fact, it didn't even occur to me to do so. On the contrary, I suppose I was, if anything, rather impatient to get on with the procedure after he had taken so much longer to complete the first stage.

One thing, he did see the front door of his mother's house very vividly and in considerable detail. I, too, have seen that door, during our return to the Netherlands in 1970; in fact I saw it several times, yet I couldn't myself remember it in anywhere near the detail that Leo now used when describing it. Furthermore, he assures me now, as I write this some five or six weeks later, that he did see it very vividly and clearly indeed, as much so as in a coloured photograph or at the cinema, and certainly much more vividly than in any dreams he had ever had. He also says that the 'memory of this memory' (to put it rather clumsily) is still, at the time of my writing, perfectly clear and a matter of some dismay and wonderment to him.

Not only could he see this door, but he described its green colour, the glass panelling in the upper half with narrow wooden divisions, and even the bell (its present one, not the more ornate one he remembers from his childhood). He says that he saw the door's surroundings too with the same vivid clarity, the brick walls with a small side window near the door, on the inside of which an ornamental vase has always stood. He could also see the small garden between the house and the street, about two yards wide, with its plants and one tall shrub which closed the garden off from that of the neighbours. Furthermore, to his surprise he also saw this neighbours' door, very similar to that of his own home, but mostly yellow with only a trimming of green, instead of his mother's completely green door.

He had no trouble either when asked to ascend to the top of the roof. He managed this very quickly and, he said, could instantly see the street at the front of the house, the petrol station and garage opposite, the houses and shops along the street, and beyond these to the parklands, which also became clearly visible to him. Turning, he could see the garden at the back of the house, the shed for firewood and bicycles, even the rubbish bins. And in the garden he could see the small rectangle of lawn, the shrubs, and the tall trees which again served to give privacy from the immediate neighbours. Looking farther away, he could see the back fence and then the neighbours' garden beyond that, their house and the houses alongside and even beyond. He could see still further, to the school in the block beyond, and the buildings and landscape even farther away.

As I naturally knew something of his life and background, I asked him if this was the school where his father had been a teacher, before he had been killed by a traffic accident just over eleven years before. He said no, it was not, but then found that he had immediately 'leapt' to that school. I did not at all want this to happen, so I tried to bring him back to the house. However, this wouldn't happen either. Nor could he ascend higher into the air even though he had not yet 'come down' to earth. Try as he would, he could not go up; but he told us that he could very clearly see the high tower of the Dom (or cathedral) of Utrecht.

He seemed simply to remain floating; and I remember that I became a little alarmed, so I told him to look clearly at the ground below him and then 'land'. He tried, but said he immediately went off over the rooftops again, travelling rapidly until, when he did eventually land, it was in Bilthoven. This is a suburb adjacent to De Bilt, but he had landed at a point some eight kilometres (about five miles) from his home. Try as I would, I couldn't get him up again. However, he was 'seeing' his home ground so vividly that I decided to let him go on.

He had landed in an area with a lot of bushes and shrubs which are the beginning, in actuality, of a small wood. It was autumn and he said that the colours were brilliant. He did not see but he *knew* that behind him was a cinema which he had frequented when he had been living at home. Before him there was a fence of netted wire and, beyond this, several country-style houses, all of which actually exist there. He saw all this, he said, as clearly as if he had really been there.

As he did not seem to be progressing, I again asked him if he could return to his home in De Bilt. At once, he told us, he found himself on the back of a motor-cycle—still in Bilthoven—being driven by a youth whom he thought was either his young brother or a German school-friend: he could not be sure which. He described the road they were travelling along until they came to a building, a very old one; once one had had to pay a toll to use the road, but this no longer applies and, since it went out of use as a toll-house, the building has been moved from one side of the street to the other. But that was all. Leo said that as he described and explained this toll-house, the motor-cycle with its cyclist just disappeared, leaving him standing alone on the road.

He felt he couldn't go on any more, and in any case was so disappointed that he hadn't been able to travel farther, let alone to a past life, that he didn't want to continue. So of course we stopped, thinking we had encountered our first failure.

But of course it wasn't a failure. When he is asked about it now, he says that even this much is one of the most vivid experiences of his life. He says that he is not much given to dreaming, or, if he does, that his dreams must be far from vivid, as he can rarely, if ever, recall them. He does not remember any, in either content or clarity, that were anywhere near as memorable as this visualization was to him; and he still hasn't forgotten a moment or any detail of his rather restricted journey. However, he says now that he is no longer apprehensive and that he will willingly try again when we are able to—so this means that I have yet another experiment to attempt and record.

Meanwhile several other experiments have been made, all with greatly varying degrees of both success (in terms of time and distance 'leaps') and clarity. Also, after Leo's first attempt, Joy contacted the woman who had written the articles in the magazine *Open Mind*, including that on travelling to past lives. This woman gave as an explanation for Leo's failure to 'return' that he had probably died a violent death in his previous life and so his spirit or 'overself' was reluctant to return to that particular life in case it should have to go through the same ordeal all over again. This seemed all too pat and glib to me. I preferred to think that Leo had simply been reluctant to give himself up fully to the experiment, and so it hadn't entirely succeeded. Explanations, reasons and excuses can hardly be expected to be proved. So far as I am concerned, I am interested only in recording what has happened to me personally or what has been recorded in my presence.

For I am already convinced at least that there is a great deal to the experiments without indulging in any artificial attempts at substantiation or even, as yet, researching into what might already have been recorded about the subject. I have no doubt—no doubt whatsoever—that the quite simple procedure I have described does indeed produce some kind of revelation, but whether or not it can be any possible 'return to a past life' I am still quite unprepared to say. Yet I cannot possibly dismiss it altogether either. And if it should prove no more than just 'taking a trip'—something so popular these days—but without resort to drugs, alcohol or even hypnotism, then this much alone is a most pleasant and illuminating experience. Moreover, during the past few weeks I have seen that a number of very different people find it so as well.

However, before I was to carry the experiment to anyone apart from the four of us, both Ray and I were to experience what happened on a second attempt.

Chapter Six

After Leo's experience, in the same evening, Ray was taken for a second trip.

There is no need for me to record the preliminary stages of the experiment with him this time other than to say that on this second occasion he managed the stretching and expanding exercises very much faster and far more easily than he had on his first attempt. And as might be expected, the memory exercises, the imagining of being up on the roof and then ascending high up into the air, were also accomplished much more quickly and easily. This time, too, it was very much easier to bring him down to land again.

At first we were a little disappointed with this experiment. I don't know why, but for some reason we had all expected Ray to return—if indeed he could manage to 'return' at all—to some other life entirely, or at least to another *period* of this previous one, and perhaps with different surroundings. But he returned almost immediately to what at first seemed to be the exact scene and period in time as previously. And as he began to describe it, it was almost like watching a second viewing of a film which was all too familiar.

There was apparently the same dark water and mountains to begin with, and once more a complete absence of people. But this time, as we realized after a while, there was no village, no sign of habitation whatsoever. I made a point of asking him this, as I had presumed him to have returned to exactly the same place and period in time as before. The period of time may have been the same, as was the general location 'somewhere in Norway'; but this time he said he was not *up in the mountains* by a lake, but was down at the sea, with mountains rearing up from the shore.

As before, it was night; and this rather disappointed him. Having had one experience during night-time, he hoped it would now be day as it had been for me and for Joy. He paused, and I saw his forehead crease quite perceptibly, and afterwards he said he had been trying to change the night to day. He *wanted* it to be daytime, but night persisted and, soon becoming resigned to it, he allowed the experience to continue as it would.

He was standing, he said, on a great granite-like slab of rock, the kind that is in actuality so much a part of the coastline in Norway. It was night-time still, but at least it was a moonlit night. Everywhere was calm and peaceful and quite beautiful to behold. He could not see it, but he sensed, or even *knew*, that the sea was behind him. I asked him how he knew this but he said he couldn't tell, it was just *there*. He had the feeling that he was even close to the water's edge, though he couldn't see the water—and no, he didn't want to turn round to look at it. He knew it was there and there were other things before him which he wanted to see. No, there were no people, and not even a sign of any anywhere. There was no sign of any habitation. He was alone—completely and rather terribly alone. He wanted to start to walk, looking for someone.

And he *was* now walking, he said, but he was still alone. He kept looking at his hands, and could see them distinctly—huge hands, even larger than they really are. As a child (he told me afterwards) he had been so conscious of the size of his hands—though they were nowhere near so big as in his previous life—that he had mostly kept them hidden in his pockets when he was in the presence of people other than his family. But in this second return, as in his previous experience, he had no family. That was why he was searching, hoping to find someone he could make his own.

He was walking through tall fir trees, he said; a dense forest of them. And it was still night-time, but still moonlight. He passed through beautiful glades with rock-forms and shrubs and even faint paths, yet he still did not see anyone. Nor was there any sound of people as there had been before; no sound whatsoever. Then he came to another lake, again one that was calm and quite black in the night. He walked along its shore between water and forest, then came to a beautiful place with a very large tree—not a fir tree this time, but one that had a huge spread of branches and was of enormous strength and thickness of bole. From near by he could hear the sound of water and, on looking in the direction of the sound, saw a small waterfall with its crystal waters tumbling into a pool, from which a stream chattered off somewhere into the distance. He said he felt content there; on the other hand, there was still no one.

And then he said, in a tone so desolate that it quite startled the three of us, and I suppose none more than his wife Joy, 'I was alone then—and I'm still alone!' It was not at all clear whether he meant that he was still alone in his present life, or that he had merely been alone in the first visualized scene he had experienced and he was still alone in the second. Somehow none of us felt like asking.

He said nothing for a while, then merely reported that everything had gone drab again. There were no 'highlights'. He had no wish to remain 'there' any longer, when this second experience also had nothing of either excitement or even consolation to offer. So he opened his eyes, sat up, and was instantly 'back'.

It had been so brief this time that he looked round at us almost apologetically.

'I think I'm too tired,' he said. 'We shouldn't have tried a second run after Leo's.'

And so, all feeling the same way, we resolved that it was really too much to have more than the one run an evening. At the same time Ray protested when I suggested that this second experience of his had been a failure. It was all perfectly vivid and clear. It was just that he had been disappointed at its happening at night again instead of by day, and also that he had felt the same desolating sense of such utter loneliness.

'If it does nothing else,' he said, 'at least it reminds me that I always *was* alone in Norway. That's why I wanted to leave the place! So maybe this is a warning...'

Warning? Recently, he said, he had had the hankering to go back there, perhaps to live. The previous year he and Joy had gone on a flying visit to Europe and had been to most countries there, including Norway. He had suddenly seen a great deal of Europe that he had missed, and had been surprised at how much it had progressed beyond his greatest expectations. In the years he had been away from it there had been more progress and growth than there has been in the same period in Australia, especially in Western Australia where he had come to make his home.

His wife, Joy, though born here, had lived for some time in Singapore, but had found even this experience insufficient to prepare her for the tremendous impact of seeing Europe for the first time. She said now that she had also felt this same discontent since returning. She would not mind if Ray was to sell up and take another appointment, as he so easily could, somewhere in Europe. Yet neither of them wished to settle in the Norway which they had both visited. They preferred either France or, more particularly, Spain. And it was still a great temptation to go there.

'So you see?' he went on. 'At least if these "returns" '—and he was quite easily, even effortlessly, able to refer to them as such—'do have a meaning to them, it's quite clear that they are both warnings to me to steer clear of Norway!'

Would that be the end of the experiment for him? No, he definitely wanted to 'go' again—and again and again. But meanwhile the rest of us had to have our turns for a second attempt. Leo didn't yet feel ready for his, and Joy said the impact of her first one was still too vivid in her mind for her to want to confuse it, perhaps, with another. So I was to be next.

Chapter Seven

Although this was to be my second attempt, it was the first time, remember, that I would experience the greater part of the visualization and memory exercises. And so, as I prepared myself for these preliminaries, I found myself in an excitement of anticipation perhaps even greater than at the first experiment, for then I had been quite sceptical about anything happening at all. Now that I knew differently, I wondered if I would be able to accomplish the preliminary exercises as both Ray and Joy had, or would I fail like Leo?

The stretching exercises were simple and, of course, familiar, and so I had no difficulty whatsoever in again stretching to a greater height and then shrinking back to normal size. Apart from the weird sensation of feeling—and I mean feel *physically*—what I was commanding my mind merely to visualize, this time I could *see* it—and see it very clearly. The extraordinary thing was that, although my shoes were removed as required for the massaging of the ankles, I still had my socks on; but the moment I closed my eyes and concentrated on my feet receding two inches for the first exercise, I could see them as vividly as if I were indeed looking at my own feet, but completely bare. I could see no socks at all. I even tried, while performing the stretching and shrinking exercise, to put socks back on to my feet, but it wouldn't work. I also realized that I couldn't remember what colour my actual socks were—nor can I now, of course. What was even more uncanny was that I was perfectly conscious of Leo's massaging my ankles, just as I was of Joy's more vigorous massaging on my forehead as she took me for the trip; but it felt as though I was being massaged *without* any socks on. Then it occurred to me that by indulging in this frivolity I could easily spoil the rest of the exercise, and so I decided to stop thinking of any such extraneous matters. Having made the decision, I stopped immediately, I now remember. But I think *now*, at the time of writing, that this was not so much due to my having instructed myself, so to speak, to stop thinking extraneous thoughts, as to the concentration demanded (and readily if not quite spontaneously given) by the ensuing exercises, particularly those involving growing taller through the head.

Yet the expanding part of the process was, for me, a different matter. I did indeed feel and actually see something of myself expanding, but still nowhere to the extent, I now think, that both Ray and Joy had.

But then Joy said, 'I want you to imagine that you are standing just outside your front door', and I was immediately there. I was even a little impatient when she asked me if I could see it, for I was instantly so absorbed in seeing my door that I had forgotten that the others, of course, couldn't possibly know that I was 'there' until I said so. It was indeed as if I were standing outside it in reality. There was not only the white wooden door itself, with the number one affixed to it centrally in the vertical sense, and at approximately my own eye-level horizontally, but even the small circular 'eye' of the 'spy-glass' lens two inches or so underneath it, so that the two together looked almost like an exclamation mark.

At first I was a little puzzled that I could not see the nickel, slightly rusted doorknob at the right-hand side of my door and about half-way up, nor the square of doorbell button with its rounded corners; but I soon stopped puzzling over this by becoming absorbed in seeing the aluminium fly-proof door in front of it, with its rather modest design. I could see the stained-wood doorstep and the doormat. Remembering this now, I have just gone outside to look and found that a horizontal aluminium bar on the wire-door completely obstructs the view of both the main door's handle and the bell. I must also say that at the time I knew what these two items should look like, even to the slight rusting from the sea-air of the circular doorknob; yet I am sure that had I been asked to describe these items prior to this experiment, I wouldn't have been able to do so. I wrote that particular 'I am sure' very deliberately, for I have just tried to remember what a particular window of my apartment looks like from the outside, and nothing nearly so vivid occurred. On the contrary, I had great difficulty in recalling any details at all, and when I went to check on what I presumed to have been a fairly good piece of recollection, I found that I had been hopelessly wrong. The lock and the length of the curtains I had 'recollected' were both totally different from reality, and it had not even occurred to me that the one side of the dual window which could be opened had a fly-proof-wired frame outside it. So in this respect, at least, the procedure could be a much more reliable form of memory. And if so, wouldn't it be a far easier and much more reliable form for the memorizing of, say, a whole room, as required for some occupations, than the deliberately conscious memorizing of individual features and contents.

But these ideas have occurred to me only after the experiment. At the time I was already anxious and curious to see what would happen to me with the exercises I had missed before.

It is extraordinary how easily and vividly one can be 'transported' from the ground to the top of the roof of one's abode—in my case from a ground-floor apartment to the flat roof of a three-storey apartment building. And when I was told to look down and around me, not only did I do so but I walked to the edges of the roof and peered over, seeing not merely what was beneath and around me but even my own feet and legs up to the hips. I even felt a touch of vertigo at first, but this soon disappeared (as it wouldn't have in real life) when I found myself fully occupied with seeing and describing everything before me—but which I still have never seen in reality from this viewpoint.

I chose the rear of the building and could immediately see the rather attractively architectured dual stairways—a pattern of geometrical lines and angles upon which most visitors invariably comment after their first encounter with them, and which amateur-photographer friends like to use as backgrounds. On either side of these were the small squares of lawn and narrow gardens of plants and shrubs. But in the centre of these lawns, occupying most of the two areas, I could not only see the square clothes-hoists which are so much a feature of Australian back gardens, but also washing drying on them. And although it was night at the time when I was visualizing this, and a winter night at that, it was daylight in my visualization—a warm, bright summer day with, as is usual in this locality, a moderate sea-breeze wafting the clothes out from the wires to which they were pegged and making the hoists turn, as they do when they are wound up sufficiently for the larger items to be well above the ground.

Then I could see the taller apartment building which is back-to-back with the one in which I live. I could see its windows and doorways and grilled connecting balconies, the open 'car-port' of aluminium roofing and even cars in other areas provided for parking underneath the building. There were people moving around—very realistic people, but none of them recognizable, which doesn't surprise me, as even now I know very few of them in reality. Looking to the right, I could see the other buildings to the landward side, with the tall spiky spires of the many Norfolk Island pine trees which have been planted here. I shall spare you all the details of what I could see; suffice it to say that these were not only clear and vivid in colour, but also incredibly accurate when I later compared them with reality. Consequently the experience was and is, to say the least, enthralling.

Turning to the front of the building, I could again see the lawns and gardens, shrubs and flowering plants, and the drive-way the width of my apartment, descending from underneath the full width of my thirty-foot-long balcony to the road. There was the brick construction for the five letter-boxes. There were the fences and homes opposite, more trees beyond them, and then the great expanse of the golf-links so inconveniently bisected by a public road, then more buildings beyond the golf-links and after them the sea and coastline stretching to the Fremantle harbour with its artificial stone moles, a veritable forest of ships' funnels and masts, the harbour buildings and the tall, almost fairy-castle-like wheat silos, and then once more the sea stretching away blue upon blue.

For now I was turning to gaze directly out to sea and I had a clear view all the way to the horizon—just as clearly as if, in reality, I had ever been up on that roof. But I haven't. Like Ray (for we live within a mile of each other), I could also see the long, low, undulating silhouette of Rottnest Island as it is visible only on a clear summer day. And if my experience from the experiment had ended then and there, this much alone would have been marvellously satisfying.

But, of course, there was the ascent to come next, and again I was amazed at how easily this was accomplished. It was much as though I was being transported directly upwards by a lift of some sort, but one without walls or bars of any kind, certainly without a roof, or even a floor for that matter. There was no sense of weight, but there was, nevertheless, a very real sense of ascension.

And below me the earth and sea and coastlines all fell away as though I was indeed making a directly vertical ascent, which none of the innumerable aeroplane flights I have made during and many times since the Second World War have ever provided. It remained daylight, of course, but only until I was told to change the scene below me from day to night, and as with Ray this immediately happened. And again as Ray had done, I could see the city of Perth and its environs for many miles, just as I have indeed seen it in reality, a magnificent pattern of both consistent and scintillating lights. I could also see the oddly shaped estuary of the Swan River, now dark and smooth at night, and the dim yet still well-defined coastline separating land from the great expanse of dark and mysterious ocean.

Then I was asked to change night back to day, and I did so —and was conscious of the fact that I must make the effort to do so; it merely remained night if I waited, as I did for a few moments, to see if it would change of its own accord.

And so it was day again, but this time something had happened. There was something very different about it, and for a short while this difference puzzled me. Then I realized what it was—clouds had appeared between me and the earth below for the very first time. Above them, the sun was brilliant, and the breath-taking panorama which the tops of the clouds made was the marvel it always is to me whenever I transcend them in an aeroplane, no matter how many hundreds of times I have experienced it. But below them I could catch only glimpses of both ocean and land. It was only when I was told to descend that, having passed through the cloud with the expected enveloping of near-impenetrable fog, I could suddenly and clearly see both the earth and sea beneath me.

But now that was all that there was—the earth and the sea: there were no houses or suburbs, city or river. The only definition in the entire panorama below me was that of the coastline steadily rising towards me as I descended, but even that was becoming slowly dimmed as the cloud above me obliterated the sun and cast a deep shade over everything below. I stated this, and was asked if I could clear the cloud in order to be able to descend in the safety of clear sunlight. But no matter how much I tried, I couldn't. I suppose Joy became a little worried, for she asked me if I would prefer to ascend again, then descend only if the sun persisted and I could clearly see the coastline. But despite her suggestions I was still descending, as though I could not stop, but at a steady rate, in silence, and without any apprehension whatsoever. For, dim as it was, I could clearly see the coastline and even the point where it looked as though I would land. There were very tall and rugged cliffs which do not exist anywhere near Cottesloe where I live in reality, and from where I had originally ascended. I was still descending, but now I was indeed becoming a little apprehensive, for what remained of the daylight was not only fading fast but the cliffs and sea where I was going to land became wilder and more formidable as I approached them. But I couldn't stop myself. And suddenly I was 'there', cold and spray-drenched, on this alien and rugged coastline with the sea roaring behind me, and night so dark that all I could see now were indeterminate faint glimmerings of light here and there in the wet black face of the cliffs towering above me.

Had I landed?

Yes, I said, and then described this quite forbidding landfall of mine.

Was I frightened being there? Did I want to return?

No, I wasn't at all frightened, for I somehow knew that I was going to be all right, although I also knew that I had to proceed with great caution.

I was quite sure I wanted to go on?

Yes, I was quite sure.

Did I know where I was?

No. I was nowhere I had ever been before. It was a completely strange and quite hostile coast.

Could I see my feet?

Yes.

Was I wearing anything on them?

No, they were bare; they were huge and bare with great

coarse and ragged toenails. My legs were thick and muscular, hairy.

What was I wearing?

Some kind of thickly furred skin. I couldn't see it clearly because it was dark in colour and it was night-time; but I could feel the skin's weight and warmth—and even, I thought, that it was damp here and there, just as I was.

Yes, I was cold; it was very cold where I was and I longed for warmth.

But yes, I could also feel the warmth on my 'present' body from the fire in the living-room where the four of us were. Yes, I was still conscious of lying there on this sitting-room floor; my hands could feel the carpet beneath my palms and I could hear the sound of the fire, and Joy's voice prompting me, the occasional traffic or other noises outside, the music from the radiogram. But as soon as I concentrated on what I could see of my new surroundings, all these distractions faded away. Yet they didn't disappear entirely; but they no longer intruded or distracted me. I was again much too absorbed...

In the dark and the cold of this wide and forbidding coastline, I was now a large and coarse kind of creature. And I was leaving—though not running from in the sense of any urgent escape—some kind of hostile environment. This I could not see; no detail would come to me, but it was sufficient that I had *chosen* to leave it and seek somewhere else to live. I was quite alone; I think I always had been. I was living at a time when, once a child was sufficiently grown to look after itself, it was cast off by its parents to make its own way in a world where survival was particularly hazardous, not only from the wild and savage animals which roamed the bleak countryside, but also from the quite bestial savageries of its fellow-men.

In this life, or visualization, however you prefer to think of it, I had not descended to this particular piece of coastline; although I still recalled the descent I had made, it was not part of the experience in which I was now participating. (In just the same manner I could be aware at a stage *twice* removed from my present reality, that I was still lying on a twentieth-century sitting-room floor.) I had *not* descended to this coastline, but had arrived at this particular point on it by having proceeded *along* the coastline from where I had lived before, not from any village but in the course of a rather nomadic existence of foraging around from place to place, almost continually hunting animals to eat, sometimes cooked—or seared, rather—over an open fire, but more often raw, drinking the blood instead of water, and often still warm from the carcass at that.

But I wanted to leave this brutal existence. I felt there was a place somewhere else where one could live much more comfortably, and where indeed a community of human beings, including some of my own community who had sought and found their way there before me, did live in comfort and with amenities beyond my knowledge or even my imagination, but which, nevertheless, I could sense. I had come to this point in the coastline because the region between where I had lived before and where I now wanted to live was of towering, precipitous, impassable mountain terrain that had not a tree, not a shrub, not a plant nor a leaf nor even the vestige of one. But at this point in the coastline, I knew from some kind of precognition, there was a 'way'.

And this 'way' soon revealed itself. As I stumbled from the ocean rearing and roaring behind me, tripping over the slippery slabs and slants of rock that were so difficult to make out in the dark, I could eventually detect a glow, a dimness of light, which seemed to shine out from the unscaleable cliff-face at its base. I did not know the name for such a thing as I now approached, but it was a tunnel.

Let me say that again. I did not 'know' with the mind with which I was equipped in the body I now possessed, but I knew it to be a tunnel with the mind which I possessed in the present self, or life, which I had temporarily (I hoped) abandoned. I didn't much care for the body and life I was now experiencing.

I had found this tunnel, one with several mouths or entrances rather like the many-tributaried deltas of some rivers. Rough pillars, broad at their bases and tops but worn slimmer at their waists, served the dual purpose of supporting the roof and dividing these several entrances one from another. The light, or steady glow, was a mystery to me—not only a mystery but a thing of wonder. It was something which my own kind was incapable of producing. Fires, yes—but this steady, consistent glow, no. And again I knew it to be a glow produced by some artificial means only from the knowledge of my present or actual mind.

Along the floor of this tunnel, which was rough and treacherous with many stones of all shapes and sizes, there was a small stream running from wherever the tunnel began towards the sea—a sea that was now well behind me, its roar gradually diminishing as I half-ran, half-trotted, sometimes stumbling, deeper into the tunnel.

Instead of it growing quickly darker as I half-expected, it remained light. It would indeed dim now and again, but only to brighten once more. And the source of all this light? It came through shafts cleft from the upper surface of the mountain—which was some great and imperceptible height above me—clean through the mountain rock to the ceiling of the tunnel. Was it bright moonlight above? I didn't think so, neither then nor now. *Now* I think—indeed, feel certain—that it was some kind of artificial light, something like electricity and yet much more advanced than even our present electric lighting. Again I had a kind of precognition that it was the accomplishment of a prior and much more civilized race that was superior even to twentieth-century man, moon-landings and all notwithstanding. But again this precognition told me that the civilization which had been responsible for this source of light had either become extinct or had departed—departed, I mean, from the face of this planet. All this I thought at the time of the experience, a factor I feel I must remind you of from time to time.

The tunnel lasted quite some distance—several miles at least, though I'm not at all sure how many. I know that I panted and sometimes had to rest, and would scoop up water from the narrow but clear little stream in the centre of the tunnel's floor; the water was cool, almost chilled, and marvellously pure of taste. I also saw my hands much more clearly—great brutal, hairy hands with nails more like claws. I was bearded and bushy, all wild with a great tangle of hair that was both dark in colour and curly to the extent of being almost fuzzy. I could see my features in the calm surface of a small backwater in the stream, and my eyes were wild and blue, though in actuality they are brown, and my lips coarse and blistered and cracked, with streaks of red flesh, almost like blood, easily detectable.

My shoulders were huge and my body almost as hairy as the fur which partly covered it, not for any sense of decency but purely as protection against the bitter cold—for I could see now that I wore the fur with the skin, crudely dried and smelling abominably, on the outside. The fur was not the only thing to smell; my own body stank. It was more like that of an animal than of a man. But there were both animals and men, I well knew, who were much cruder and far more savage than I. And it was from these I wanted to escape.

So on I stumbled, half running, half trotting, I don't know for how long. But eventually the shafts of light from above came to an end and I could make out a more familiar, if only faint, glow, appearing far away. There, I knew, was the end of the tunnel. Yet when I eventually reached this other opening, on the other side of the mountains through which the tunnel had been dug by highly accomplished men of a much earlier period in the world's existence, it was still night. I had to fumble my way through near-darkness, staggering all the more and frequently stubbing my toes and barking my shins painfully against obtruding rocks.

Then I emerged. I was, as I expected, on the other side of the mountains, on the other side of the island. There was the sea again before me—a sea still dark, but much calmer than that which I had just left. To the right, or the north, the mountain cliffs plunged straight down into the sea so that the coast was quite impassable, for which I was enormously relieved. Unless they also found and followed the tunnel, these fellow-men whom I never wanted to see again would not be able to come to this part of the island.

To the left, in the near-black dark, I could just detect a small village with a low fire burning, against which I could pick out dim shapes of people moving around. I had to push myself from the cliff-face, where I had been leaning and panting, to stumble on towards it. After a while I could see small, round huts, made of mud and rushes or bark, but mostly mud. They were very primitive in construction, or at least so one part of my mind told me, while the other knew that the construction of even these primitive shelters was a sheer marvel that was not yet part of my knowledge. Yet somehow I *expected* a village of such huts, built by a people still primitive by my actual standards but very advanced compared with my visualized self and those other people I had just left.

As I approached, one of these new people saw me. I stopped,

just as he had. I watched carefully, for now this figure was gesturing at others in the village to look in my direction. They did, and I felt sudden alarm. But then, after a moment or so, the first figure I had seen made a gesture which I knew was beckoning me to approach and join them. I was still a little apprehensive; but on the other hand, wasn't this exactly what I had come for? And so I went on towards them.

I reached them. They were all around me. I could see their faces clearly, and the skins they wore. Their faces were vastly different from my own, though still, of course, those of human beings. These people were raw-boned and coarse-featured, with huge staring eyes and large protruding teeth. My *present* mind was immediately reminded of the faces in Van Gogh's 'The Potato Eaters'. They were really quite fearsome faces, I suppose; yet they did not frighten me. They were smiling—rather tentative smiles, admittedly—but they *were* indeed smiling and again beckoning me to join them, making gestures and expressions of both acceptance and welcome.

I was enthralled by their huts. Crude constructions though they were, no higher than my own height and with only a small aperture for entry through which one had to crawl, they were nevertheless marvels to me. I patted them with my huge hands, feeling the rough texture of the walls; and yet this roughness was an amazing smoothness to me.

And I was enthralled with the people. They were kind, as my own people had never been. They were hard-working, too, as my own people had never been. For these people had also achieved agriculture. They pointed to their crops alongside their huts, and then to the fire which had drawn me to them in the first place. Over the fire they had cooking utensils such as I had never seen before: great stone vessels in which they cooked a kind of gruel. They also ate fish and seabirds, which they caught themselves with nets for the fish and small bows and arrows for the seabirds. And these they cooked in the coals of the fire, tending to them and removing them when cooked with sticks about the length of walking-sticks, but which had formerly been the narrower branches of trees broken off at the trunk, so that a small angular piece of the trunk was left on one end to serve as a kind of fork for scooping the cooked fish and seabirds out from the fire.

I was given some to eat. They laughed when I had to toss

the food from hand to hand, sucking at my burnt fingers. But when I could eventually eat it, I marvelled at its taste and also at that of the gruel. This was sometimes scooped up in smaller, round stone vessels, which I could now see that they had somehow carved themselves. But they would also sometimes pour some of the gruel on to a hot, smooth and level stone in the fire. To my amazement it cooked and rose into a kind of bread, or damper, which was even more delicious to eat.

But the greatest marvel to me was that these people made sounds which obviously had meanings for each other. One would make sounds, and then another, or others, would not only understand the meaning of these sounds but make other meaningful sounds in return. Instinctively I knew this to be 'language', which my own kind had not yet accomplished. I wondered at it, yet it did not dismay me. On the contrary, I somehow knew that my own people had not yet evolved this civilized and complex method of communication because our way of life was still too primitive and too hard; it did not provide the time for such refinements to be even conceived, let alone acquired. I had come to a community where life was much less hostile and primitive—and hence to this marvel of language.

As though this were not enough, I was then taken and shown implements kept at the edge of the field, but still within the light from their fire. They demonstrated to me how to use these implements to dig the ground and make furrows. Already I was almost pathetically anxious to please these new people around me and started to dig and furrow furiously. But to my dismay someone took hold of my arm to stop me and the man I had first seen was again gesturing to me. He was indicating that I should follow him, and so of course I did.

He led me to one of the huts in the village, then pointed to its small entrance and made signs to me to go in. At first I could hardly believe such generosity, but I could see that my benefactor not only meant what he was gesturing but that the rest of the community was eagerly watching to see my reactions to what was to me an act of great welcome and generosity. I looked from face to marvellous if ugly face, then did not hesitate any longer. Dropping to my hands and knees, and feeling the ground firmly beneath both, I then lowered myself further till my body was pressed flat on the earth. Then I wriggled myself inside.

At first, of course, I couldn't see. But soon my eyes became accustomed to the dark and I discovered that there was practically nothing to see in any case—merely a 'bed' which was really only straw and leaves heaped against the far wall of the hut. I crawled over to them and then, turning myself round, lay down on them with the curve of my back fitting snugly against the curve of the far wall.

From here I could see directly outside the small entrance, so the ground beyond and the feet and lower legs of some of my benefactors were visible to me. And then suddenly so also were some of their faces, grinning widely as they lowered themselves to look at me inside, each one laughing with approval at my having guessed the function of the hut and making noises of meaning to each other which, to me, was still the greatest marvel of all about them. I knew that I would have to learn these noises—this language—but I also knew that I would, merely by being able to use their language, have so much more knowledge and appreciation of life.

I was in a strange land, with a strange people—but I was home...

Then the scene dimmed, my eyes flickered, the sounds and voices of the three people who had been listening to all this drowned the voices of those other people I had reached, and I was back.

Not only was I back but, as in my first experience, I had the meaning of this journey, too, quite firmly in my mind. If in my first return I had become aware of the limitations of hieroglyphics as a form of written communication, this second return could not have been more effective in making me aware of how desolate life would be without language at all. Did I need any other lesson than these to send me scuttling back to my typewriter? Could anything but these revelations have been more effective—or even half as effective—in producing these convictions?

And if the whole experience had simply been an entertainment, then this alone would have been more than enough to give satisfaction—and so much more satisfaction than anyone could expect from so simple and inexpensive a procedure.

Chapter Eight

Although there were still two of us, Joy and Leo, to make a second attempt I already felt that I should like to try the experiment on people outside our own small group of four. And I found that as soon as I suggested this, and told a little of what happened or was supposed to happen, most were willing to try it especially when assured that no harm could come to them. If they were not willing to participate, they were at least curious. But before I started experimenting with other acquaintances several rather uncanny references to the matter itself cropped up.

The first arose because Joy had a birthday in July when we were trying this Christos Experiment. As one of her particular interests connected with her work is architecture, I was pleased to find a beautiful volume about it only just published. Naturally I glanced through it before wrapping it up to give to her, and was astounded almost immediately upon opening it to be confronted by a sketch of a village of white and circular houses almost exactly like those which I had seen in my first experience. Furthermore, in the centre of this village—or my own first city as it seemed to me—was a larger, two-storey circular and dome-roofed building which, of course, belonged to the community's 'leader'. As this volume aspires to cover all the world's architecture through all its ages, there was not a great deal of information given about this particular early type of structure. Indeed, all that was given read as follows:

> *Khirokitia in Cyprus.* Neolithic village of circular houses. The circular, domed structure, whether of brick or snow blocks, is one of the primary structural forms that persist until the present day.

Cyprus—not somewhere in the upper reaches of the Nile as I had instinctively surmised. But then again, the matter of these structures 'persisting until the present day in Iraq and Iran, or one of man's oldest civilizations around the Tigris and Euphrates rivers', as well as being one of man's primary structural forms, did not exclude them from having been located in the Sudan as well. Indeed, very likely this had been the kind of dwelling, and collection of dwellings forming a village, which I had seen. Furthermore, from the description I had given of them at the time, none of us had any doubts when I showed this sketch in the book that this was indeed the very environment I had visited.

There was only one dismaying aspect of this discovery, and that was that the time of this first visit of mine had been several thousand years before Christ, instead of perhaps only the centuries that I had then surmised. My second visit had, of course, been even earlier, probably again by several thousand years. Why should this have been so much of a surprise? Well, in the first place I had really expected such returns, if they were to occur at all, to have been only to a few centuries ago, not millennia. And if there hadn't been any other incarnations between, where then had my spirit or overself been in those 'between times'?

But there was an even more dismaying point. When telling other friends something of the experiment and the experience it produced, I was promptly handed a copy of one of Dame Daphne du Maurier's novels: *The House on the Strand*. For those who have not read it, the story concerns a man in this present day and age who, through a drug administered by a medical friend, returns several times to a previous time, but to only one particular previous time some centuries ago. The extraordinary thing about this particular work of Daphne du Maurier's, however, is not merely the ingenuity of her plot but her description of the narrator's 'return' at the very opening of the book, which is as follows:

> The first thing I noticed was the clarity of the air, and then the sharp green colour of the land. There was no softness anywhere. The distant hills did not blend into the sky but stood out like rocks, so close that I could almost touch them, their proximity giving me that shock of

surprise and wonder which a child feels looking for the first time through a telescope. Nearer to me, too, each object had the same hard quality, the very grass turning to single blades, springing from a younger, harsher soil than the soil I knew.

> I had expected—if I had expected anything—a transformation of another kind: a tranquil sense of well-being, the blurred intoxication of a dream, with everything about me misty, ill-defined; not this tremendous impact, a reality more vivid than anything hitherto experienced, sleeping or awake. Now every impression was heightened, every part of me singularly aware: eyesight, hearing, sense of smell, all had been in some way sharpened.*

This much alone would be sufficient for my purpose; however, dealing more specifically with her protagonist, the account continues:

> All but the sense of touch: I could not feel the ground beneath my feet...
>
> I was walking downhill towards the sea, across those fields of sharp-edged silver grass that glistened under the sun, for the sky—dull, a moment ago, to my ordinary eyes—was now cloudless, a blazing ecstatic blue.

Uncanny as it is, this piece of an author's imaginative prowess is exactly like my own two experiences from the Christos procedure. I had not previously encountered this particular novel, and so perhaps there may even be numerous other such descriptions in the works of other writers. But as yet I see no point in extensive research into the matter, for I feel that whatever can be experienced personally, or simply witnessed personally of acquaintances' experiences, will be far more valid than all the references to the most scholarly works on the subject.

So on to the experiences of four other people. Although they chance to have been all men, they were very different from each other in character, occupation, interests and environmental circumstances. Yet each had similar though at the same time quite differing experiences.

* Daphne du Maurier, *The House on the Strand* (Victor Gollancz, London, 1969.)

One last small but interesting point: Chambers *Twentieth Century Dictionary* gives the derivation of Joy's previous given name of 'Minna' as being Germanic and meaning 'memory or love'.

Chapter Nine

The next experience was to give concern right from the beginning, and also our first possible glimpse into the future instead of reverting to a possibly past incarnation.

Stephan M– at the time of the experiment was twenty-one and a half years of age, a welder by trade though in the past he has worked at many jobs from pipe-spinning in a stove and bath-tub factory, to general labouring, to being an assistant cook in an hotel. He was born in a small West Australian country town more than a hundred miles south of our small and isolated city of Perth. Through no fault of his own, but due mainly to his father's desertion of his mother when he was a child, he had very little schooling there. His speech is quite ungrammatical although, since our acquaintance, beginning when he was just eighteen, he has tried to correct the habitual errors he makes. At the same time, however, I have done my best to convince him first, that what one has to say matters more than how one says it and, secondly, that in his case, his way of speaking adds to his charm. He shares a flat with another welder a few years older than he, keeping his 'home' meticulously tidy. He has an instinctive eye for beauty in nature, even to forms in rocks, driftwood or sea-smoothed glass. He has not been overseas, but he has taken trips alone to the eastern states of Australia. He is both friendly and yet a little introvert, liking most people and, naturally, being liked in return. One would hardly credit that, when he had just turned eighteen, he suffered a fit of such deep depression that he attempted suicide. But, having survived, he affirms that he will never be inclined to do such a thing again.

The experiment was tried one afternoon in my apartment, not his flat, and it was tape-recorded. He was wearing jeans and a shirt but was bare-footed. In the background of the tape I hear that music was playing—Ravel's 'Daphnis and Chloe' for most of the time. Only the three of us—Stephan, Leo and myself—were present.

Stephan was a little slow with the preliminary stretching and shrinking exercises but, by the time he had reached the stage where he was required to expand, he was managing at what I had come to accept as an average rate. The memory exercises were very much easier and he required little prompting. His progress into the more imaginative visualization of ascension was also managed with little effort. He could, as well, change from day to night and back to day with ease, stating that it was he himself who effected these changes before 'descending'.

He 'landed' in a field in the country far from the coastline or Perth City or the Swan River, all of which he had previously seen so vividly by both day and night. But when he landed and was asked to look at his feet (bare in actuality) and describe what he saw, he said he was wearing shoes which were ordinary modern brown shoes with buckles (which in real life he possessed); then long white socks (which he did not actually have), a pair of Australian-type dress-shorts of black-and-white check (which he had never owned), and lastly a white, short-sleeved shirt, buttoned up (which again he did not own). This was not at all like his actual long-sleeved shirt. He wore no singlet underneath, he said. It was summer (and, of course, in actuality it was winter, but he was at least indoors with heating); he was quite warm. As he spoke, his normally quiet voice became even more subdued, to almost a whispered monotone. He remained very nearly completely inert and relaxed.

He had landed in a field in the country that was rich with green, green grass, he said. He could see every blade as though it were magnified (as in Daphne du Maurier's description which I had not at that time encountered). In the field he said there were a few cows; he spoke so softly that I at first mistook this for 'cars', but when a few more questions revealed this mistake on my part to him, he soon corrected me. There were no other people there and no other animals. There were no bushes or flowers in the field, only the grass which was 'quite long, about twelve inches high'.

He was walking around, but without any particular aim; 'just looking around', he said. There were precisely eight cows grazing near by. They were not his cows and he did not know to whom they belonged. The field itself was such a 'general' kind of field that he didn't think he had ever been there before. The only other thing he could see was a fence, a wire fence with a string of barbed wire at the top and posts of rough-hewn wood. The fence was to keep the cows in. Beyond the fence there was more grass. He didn't know if the land belonged to anyone; he could not see any farmhouse; it was all just 'a big meadow' ('meadow' in itself being an unusual word for an Australian to use instead of the much more usual 'paddock'; it was a particularly unusual word for Stephan).

There were now a few trees around, white ones, by which he meant a kind of white-trunked gum-tree. There were still no other animals, people, or even birds. It was the present time, he thought, but he was adamant that he had never been in this place before. Yet he could see it, he said, as clearly as if it were indeed real and also in broad daylight. He didn't even have any idea where it might be, except that he thought it was *somewhere* in Western Australia. (In fact he lived in a flat in the suburbs of Perth.) He hadn't seen this particular field before.

He didn't know what he was doing there and didn't particularly want to stay there. He wanted to go home, he said, but didn't know how he was expected to get there. He supposed he must walk.

When asked again what he was wearing, it was all as before, only the brown buckled shoes being in his actual possession. He said there was nothing on his hands, neither ring nor watch, when in actual fact he was wearing both. In his 'visualization' pocket he had about two dollars and nothing else. The notes were just loose in his pocket, he said, not in any wallet. He didn't even have a handkerchief. He had no hat. His hair was brown and 'shortish'. He had no beard or moustache, when in actual fact he was wearing a recently-grown moustache. But then came a surprise: asked how old he was, he said he was about seventeen years of age (instead of twenty-one).

He was not particularly happy where he was; he wanted to go home but he couldn't get over the fence or through its wire.

He could see no gate, and there was nobody there to help him. He didn't know how he had got into the field, but when I asked him if he remembered how he had got there, by descending to it from a visualized height in the air, he instantly remembered this. And when I asked him if he could rise again as he had done before in his visualization exercises, he immediately said, with obvious relief, that he could. And almost immediately he did.

He could both move away from where he had been and change from day to night again as he had before, seeing 'a few lights' as he had previously. Then he changed back to day again for another descent.

This time he could see land, sea and a coastline. He concentrated on a point of this coastline to land where there was a flat beach with fine white sand. There were now a few clouds which made the day dull. It took him about a minute to descend on to the beach, watching carefully where he put his feet. He was now barefooted, he said, and could feel the sand cold under his feet. The sun was behind clouds but it wasn't raining.

There were a few houses about four hundred yards away, inland. He was now wearing a pair of black football shorts and a T-shirt. He had nothing on his hands (again neither wristwatch nor ring) and he was not going to swim but merely walk along the beach because he wore only underpants under his shorts, not a swimming costume. Although there was no one with him, there were a few people there who were wearing swimming costumes. They were all married couples, he thought. Some were swimming and others just sitting on the beach. There were about a dozen people altogether, but now they were some distance off. They could possibly see him if they wanted to, but they were taking absolutely no notice of him whatsoever, and now he was walking away from them.

He continued walking along the beach which was one he did not know and was quite sure he had never seen before. The land beyond the beach was covered with low shrubs and there were a few small wooden beach cottages here and there. He couldn't see any people but he knew that there were people living there. He, however, didn't live there. He was just going for a walk for a while, and then would go back home.

The sea was becoming choppy and the sky duller. He thought

he should return but he wanted to walk a little longer. He was still wearing only a white T-shirt and black football shorts. But now he was *twenty-seven* years old! Yes, he was quite sure—he was twenty-seven years old.

After a while he said he quite liked being where he was this time, alone on the beach, and just walking, but now he wanted to go home. He wasn't sure where he lived; somewhere in a city, he thought. *His name was John.* He was quite sure of it. But now he thought he didn't have a home. And it was all some years ago.

In actuality, he now became rather distressed. His voice was very soft and almost childlike, and for one awful moment I thought he was going to cry. So I decided to 'take' him away from this location and, when I said so, his face showed obvious relief as he 'ascended' again.

This time he landed in the city of Perth, during daytime, but in a suburb. The suburb was quite clear to him; it was Karrakatta and he was landing near the cemetery which occupies most of this actual suburb. Here in Perth even the name is synonymous with death and the cemetery.

He had landed in the grounds and was at a funeral. He did not know whose funeral it was. There were about fifty people attending it. Yes, he did know some of them, 'just a few'. He could see his brother, his two sisters, and both his real father and his stepfather. It had actually happened, this funeral, he said; but when I asked him when it had happened, he said that it *had* happened, *but not yet.*

His brother and sisters were older than they now were in actuality; and he himself, standing with them, was also older. They were not talking to each other but just standing there looking at the coffin at the graveside.

He now thought that the funeral *was* of someone he knew. He was now definitely himself, Stephan, and no longer 'John', but he was now twenty-four. He was wearing a black suit and was holding a black hat in his hand. He did not possess either suit or hat in reality, but he had bought them when he was in England. In fact, he has never been to England, but was planning at the time (mid-1971) to go the following year, when he would be twenty-two years of age. He now said nothing for a while, but soon it was again apparent that he was becoming distressed—and so, by this time, was I. I decided to bring him 'back' and he 'returned' instantly and with what seemed obvious relief.

However, he was still troubled, and even after I had suggested that he stand up and move around, he still just lay there. I asked him how long he thought he had been lying there and he said 'about an hour' which was very nearly right; he had taken a little more than an hour altogether.

He could remember everything he had seen in both vivid detail and colouring. He remembered the field and then the beach and then the funeral. He knew that he had been three *different* persons, himself twice but at the different ages of seventeen and twenty-four. When he was 'John' he had been twenty-seven, but some years ago. Yet it was all, he thought, in approximately the present time. It had *not* enthralled him at all; on the contrary, he had found it rather boring and, if anything, upsetting, since he hadn't been able to 'get' anywhere.

But then came the shattering thing. When asked if he had any idea whose funeral it had been, he immediately said 'yes' without any hesitation whatsoever. It had—or rather it *would* be—his mother's funeral, he said. This was why both his father and his stepfather were there, as well as his brother and sisters. It would be in about three years' time, and naturally it distressed him to a considerable extent. On the other hand, he seemed to accept it as inevitable. No, he didn't know if his mother had any illness at the present time from which she could possibly die. Perhaps she would have an accident, he didn't know, but he thought he would ask her to go to a doctor for a check-up. Then, and this was really shattering, he suddenly said, 'But that wouldn't do any good, would it? It's going to happen...'

I asked him if he had ever been slightly clairvoyant and he said no, although sometimes he did get a hunch about things going to happen, especially if it was anything unpleasant, but no more than anyone else did, he thought. He didn't want to try the experiment again, not for a while. But if he did, he hoped he would be able to go back to something both more pleasant and more interesting. I decided not to ask him to try the experiment again and to make sure he was in much better spirits should he himself ask to try it. So far he hasn't done so.

* See note at end of next chapter, p. 87.

Chapter Ten

After this experience of Stephan's, I was reluctant to continue with any more experiments. However, I had already told something of the matter to another older and maturer friend who was still anxious to try it for himself, so eventually we decided to do so. While we were in the middle of the experiment in my apartment, we were disturbed by the unexpected arrival of another friend, whom Leo admitted, and who became a silent but fascinated witness. The person undergoing the experiment was not for one moment distracted, and he said afterwards that although he was quite aware of the other person's arrival, he was too fascinated with his experience to let anything interrupt it.

David K— who was at the time about to turn thirty-six years of age, is a highly specialized motor mechanic with his own business; he was married when he was about thirty, the marriage lasting for three years before terminating with his wife's desertion and finally divorce. At the time of the experiment he was living temporarily with his parents but preparing to rent a sizeable flat when one became available. Not just any flat would do for him; he wanted one in a particular building with spectacular harbour views and was prepared to wait for it, especially as his parents were away indefinitely touring Australia by car and caravan.

As a child, he had been a friend of one of my younger brothers years ago, but it was not until he went to work in Singapore where I was then a stockbroker that he became known to me. After only a year there, he returned to Western Australia. For some years he held a responsible position as camp manager for a large American mining concern in the north of Western Australia, some 1,500 miles north of Perth, where he would spend six months of the year during the 'dry' season when mining operations were possible, and the other six months in the Perth office organizing supplies and other necessities for the following season. He gave up this position for the sake of his marriage, but when the latter failed he acted upon a lifelong desire to own his own automotive repair business, which is now thriving.

He is a very practical and capable person with, at the same time, widely ranging interests, from motor racing to the arts, of which he has a considerable knowledge. He once allowed himself to be hypnotized and this was reasonably successful; however, he afterwards asserted that this experience was not nearly as vivid as his experience with the Christos Experiment.

During hypnotism, which he underwent with other volunteers who had varying degrees of success, he had been told that he was at the South Pole. He had immediately started to shiver, as had most of the others. When they were all told that they were at the Equator, most of the others had immediately stopped shivering and had started to sweat, and even to go through the motions of being discomforted by heat. However, he hadn't. He had continued to shiver for some time until, after several promptings, the hypnotist had eventually been successful in persuading him that he had indeed been transported to the Equator. At least his shivering had stopped, but he thinks he failed to break out in a sweat.

With this experiment, he attained relaxation with ease and was soon very proficient at stretching, shrinking and expanding. His memory exercise of the front door and its surroundings of his parents' suburban home was accomplished with quite extraordinary detail. This also applied with his being up on the roof, where he had indeed been in actuality but not for many years, nor right on the 'top' of the roof—and especially not, he maintained, just to gaze around. As I saw several days later by daylight, his assessment of the varying heights of the tall trees in the front and back gardens as well as in the surrounding neighbourhood, and the heights of surrounding houses, was quite extraordinary.

He had difficulty, however, with ascending, and this surprised me. He could ascend to a certain extent, but only with difficulty and nowhere near to the height that several others achieved with ease. He could change from day to night and back to day and, as had become customary with most others, held that he effected these changes himself.

After finding that I could not get him to ascend more than about five hundred feet or so—and if he descended he seemed invariably to return to the same point on the roof of his parents' home—I thought that perhaps there was some reason for this inability of his to ascend and, after the experience with Stephan, that we had better end the experiment. However, he wanted to continue even if he went on seeing only the immediate surroundings of his home. This, he said, was fascinating enough in itself, if nothing more were accomplished.

So I tried again several times to have him ascend, but each time he only attained a low height and descended to the same point on the roof of the house—until quite unexpectedly I realized that he was at last 'away'.

He had not managed to return to any past life, or so it seemed to me. Indeed, he hadn't even managed to land. He was flying, he thought in an aeroplane, but couldn't be sure—there wasn't any evidence of an aeroplane. And if there were, then it must have been either very small or very old, and possibly both, because of the speed (or, rather, lack of it) which he was experiencing. Also he was not, even now, at any great altitude.

But he could see all around and below him, he said, as clearly as in actuality. Indeed, what he saw was much more vivid and richly coloured, almost dazzling with brilliant sunlight on the hills and plains and rocky outcrops which stretched from horizon to horizon. Immediately below him he could see miles and miles of luxurious grass and, when he descended low enough by flying close to the ground, he was dismayed by the clarity of almost every blade of grass. Hills in the distance seemed much nearer or clearer than in reality, because of the clarity of the air which made physiographical delineations so sharp.

He recognized the country as being in the north of Western Australia where he had once worked and had flown over a good many times, but this was no particular area he could recognize.

He was quite alone. There was no sign of any habitation or other human beings, either whites or aboriginals, or even of animals, no matter where he looked. He was most definitely 'flying' around and he found the sensation of speed and pulling out of dives just above ground-level to be very exhilarating. Yet he still couldn't see any aeroplane nor even any part of himself. He could see no controls and did not think he needed them. Yet he ignored any suggestion from me that he might be a bird or some kind of spirit, he was too absorbed in his sensation of speed and seeing such vivid landscapes.

He continued flying for so long that I myself began to feel exhausted and just a little alarmed that he might 'crash' into one of the hilltops he said he was 'buzzing'. He must have indeed been doing this from the all-too-graphic descriptions he gave in rapid and excited tones which showed not the slightest sign of tiring. His voice had assumed the tone of one describing an actual flying experience in the fullest possible detail. And he continued for quite some time. No matter what I might suggest or how I might try to induce him to land, or at least bring about a change of scene, he took not the slightest notice of me. And this in itself I found quite alarming. I was already vowing 'never again'.

But eventually he did indeed start to land, though I was beginning to despair of his doing so and did not realize for a while that he was descending. He had come over a lake, he said, surrounded by many, many poplar trees. No, he had never seen the lake before and did not know whether it existed or not. But it was a very 'real'-looking lake, as were the poplar trees, and he wanted to go down to examine it more closely, especially now that he could see buildings as well.

There were many buildings, he said—tall, elongated buildings which appeared to him as though he were looking through the 'fish-eye' lens of a camera. Moreover, these buildings and the poplar trees kept *growing* towards him, as he descended to land.

He landed in the centre of a highly spectacular forest of poplar trees which stretched away in long and perfectly straight lines in all directions, and in the marvellously symmetrical patterns of rubber trees in Malayan plantations which, come to think of it, both of us had seen in actuality. But no, he had never seen poplar trees like this at any time, anywhere.

But then the poplar trees slowly changed into a huge cathedral, some of the trees changing into the cathedral's pillars while the others spread and leaned outwards from him on either side at a fantastic angle of 45 degrees. Both pillars and leaning trees, he said, formed the most incredible aisle imaginable; indeed he said he himself could not possibly imagine it, and had never seen anything like it, or even anything to suggest it.

He then started to walk along this aisle towards the altar of the cathedral and was enraptured with the magnificent wood-carvings on the pillars, as well as those on the panelled ceiling far above him. Not only were there such marvellous wood-carvings, but the texture and patterns of the wood itself were splendid, he said. Much of it was made up of a kind of semi-spherical carving which he had never seen in actuality. And as exciting as had been his experience of flying, the visual impact of these magnificent carvings was easily, he said, the most fascinating part of the whole experience. Indeed, he would have gone on rhapsodizing about it, I felt quite certain, had I not insisted upon 'bringing him back'—and he still continued enthusiastically describing the splendour of these wood-carvings; he said he had never had such an experience before.

Eventually I was able to intervene to ask him if he knew how long he had been 'away'. He thought between ten minutes and a quarter of an hour altogether, when really he had been very nearly an hour and a half. Yes, he very much wanted to try the experiment again. He said he felt now that he might be able to manage a successful return to a past life, having experienced so much this time. In any case, he very much wanted to try.

Later, just before writing this, I asked him if he had resolved for himself whether or not he had actually been in an aeroplane, and had it been the present time. He said he thought there hadn't been an aeroplane. It hadn't even occurred to him that there might be one until I myself had suggested it during the experiment. He had then looked for controls, but hadn't been surprised at not finding any. Yes, he *might* have been a bird, but some very large bird; or else, simply, and as he himself preferred to think of it, just *himself*—or his 'overself' or 'spiritual self' if I wished to think of it in that way. To him the term didn't matter. He had 'been' there and seen and done everything he had described.

When I suggested that he had merely remained in the present time, he retorted that he wasn't so sure—it could have been, say, two hundred years ago if only because he had not seen even a glimpse of people, habitation, or any sign of life, and certainly none of the enormous mining operations and cattle-stations he knew to be there now.

'I've never seen the country like that,' he said. 'In fact I've never seen *that* particular piece of country. But I'll tell you what—I'd recognize it straight away if I was ever to see it again.'

Some weeks later, I showed him the opening of Daphne du Maurier's *The House on the Strand*, which he hadn't read, and he said, yes, the sharpness of detail and colour as the writer had described it was exactly how it had been in his experience. But the rest of the book, he said, bore no resemblance, so far as he was concerned, to his own particular first experience—though there might be more similarities if he should manage to get away further, and particularly back into a past life, as he so much hoped he could.

And so I was again encouraged to continue the experiment with others, and have been asked by David several times when I would be able to give him a second run. But now for the next person's experience.

Author's note in August 1974: Stephan did go to England in 1971 for eighteen months, but returned because his mother was taken dangerously ill with a spinal disease. Fortunately, she recovered and Stephan has lived with her since, telling me their relationship has never been so close. The three years have passed and there was no funeral; he deliberately did *not* buy a suit while in England. His mother again enjoys very good health.

Chapter Eleven

David B— was a Queenslander of almost twenty-two years of age, studying law at Queensland University in Brisbane, but was on vacation with a mutual friend in Perth. He has since returned to Queensland to continue his studies.

He was immediately willing, indeed eager, to try the experiment as soon as he had been told something about it, and it was performed at night in the flat where he was staying. His host and Leo were in attendance, while I took him for the run. He lay on the floor of the flat's sitting-room with table lamps switched on, an electric radiator warming the room, and a record-player nearby playing softly.

He had no trouble with the stretching and shrinking exercises and said he was quite 'impressed' with the sensation of expanding all over. He spoke most of the time in his quiet, rather matter-of-fact tones and, as might be expected of someone following legal studies and ambitions, was meticulous over details. He 'memorized' the front door of the flat we were all in at the time, and not that of his own home some three thousand miles away, with quite incredible detail, mentioning some characteristics that neither Leo nor I, frequent visitors to the flat, nor the host himself, was aware of until we all looked after the experiment was over.

He then performed the ascending and descending visualization exercises with just as much amazing detail, particularly of a city and its environs which he was merely visiting. He could also switch easily from day to night and back to day again. When he descended, however, he found himself back in 'Queensland country' in that state's 'outback' and no longer in Western Australia. He was quite certain of this, he said, although he had never seen the particular part of country in which he had landed. He at first thought the time to be the present, but afterwards decided that it could just as easily have been anything from fifty to a hundred years ago, and was more likely to have been just before the turn of the century. When asked why he thought this, he said it was because he was walking through a typical Australian small outback town with wooden houses and buildings on either side, *but there were no electric lamp-poles*, nor any cars. Horses and carts and similar vehicles were in use. Clothing on the people he could see in the village was of an indeterminate country style, but he himself was dressed in only a pair of shorts and a singlet. He thought he was bare-footed, although at one time he could see that he was wearing a pair of boots, very old ones, without socks.

He did not live in this village. He lived alone in a small wooden cottage some five or six miles outside the village, with trees and paddocks all round him and a small stream running nearby. The cottage was so small that it had just the one room. Inside there was a stone fireplace and chimney with a fire burning, a rough camp bed, a 'safe' for food, a table with two chairs and a few shelves with some books—and nothing else. It was a dark interior even though he had seen the town and countryside in brilliant sunshine. He was astounded at the vivid colours and sharp delineations of everything he saw, in or out of doors, and at the way of life he automatically knew he followed.

For instance, he said he went once a week into the village to collect supplies, sometimes walking, sometimes with 'horse and trap'. He was always accompanied by his dog, a sand-coloured mongrel bitch that was his only companion and never left his side. His own name was Peter (not David, as in actuality) and he was about twenty-seven (instead of twenty-one) years of age. He had come to live there from the city because he wanted to get away from family and relations, and had 'found peace' in this isolated country cottage of his. He lived very simply and humbly as his needs were few. He grew most of his vegetables and fruit and reared and slaughtered sheep to eat, or so he thought. He was not at all lonely although he would like to have had a companion there with him, another bachelor like himself; he didn't want to be involved with wife and children. Otherwise he was idyllically happy and would stay there till he died.

When the experience was over, there were two unusual things about it so far as he was concerned. One was that, in this one case, we did not tell him beforehand that the aim and purported result of the experiment was to see himself in a previous life, nor was he told that this previous life might have some circumstance or condition which would pertain to some similar problem in this present life.

When asked who he thought he had been, he automatically said 'myself' but that he must have been 'in a different body'; also it had all been some years ago, maybe seventy or eighty. When told what relevance the experiment might have, he immediately said, 'Oh yes, I'd go along with that.' On the other hand, he was not at all dismayed by it, other than by the clarity and vividness of the experience; he had seen or experienced nothing like it before.

When asked how long he thought he had been performing the experiment, he was quite sure it was only about a quarter of an hour altogether, five minutes of preparation and ten minutes of the experience. He was not only incredulous at being told that it had taken an hour and a quarter altogether, he at first refused to believe it, immediately consulting his wristwatch. He then thought that one of us had altered his watch during the experience, and went to consult another clock. He was dumbfounded when eventually he was convinced, by all our watches as well, that it had indeed taken an hour longer than he thought.

He had, he said, been quite aware of his actual surroundings during most of the experience, but on the other hand he wasn't at all sure of this awareness having applied for 'the whole time', because he had been so absorbed and fascinated by the experience itself.

At the time, I myself could see no particular 'message' or reason for his having seen this past life, if past life it were—this experience of his having been the most recent by far of any of our experiments to date. But, quietly yet firmly, he contradicted me—he said it was all too plain that he was now following a career on which his heart was not set, and that he shouldn't attempt to be a lawyer working in a city at all. He would finish his studies, he said, but try to use them to work and live somewhere in the country or, better still, on the coast, away from any cities or even large towns, for he hated city life. If necessary, although he would be qualified as a lawyer, he might abandon law altogether if he could find some work he preferred, even some kind of farming. To supplement the money he had for this particular holiday in Western Australia, he had worked for some of the time as a labourer for the railways department—and he had liked it. He said he had never before been so fit and healthy and full of life and the enjoyment of living, and if that wasn't plain enough message for him, the experimentee, then nothing would be!

I think he left Western Australia as one of the most convinced and fervent devotees the experiment could have.

Author's note in August 1974: David returned to complete his studies and does now practise law—in a capacity which takes him around the countryside instead of being in a city.

Chapter Twelve

If this previous experiment with David B— had been attempted with the deliberately frivolous attitude of seeing if it would work when the person being run had no idea of what the aim of the experiment was, then the experiment to follow was attempted with the much more antagonistic attitude of thwarting it from its very beginning—or even before, if it comes to that.

Eight of us had hired a houseboat on an estuary some fifty miles or more south of the city to have what is so popular, in this part of the world at least: a week-end 'stag' party. Eight males of various ages and sizes, occupations and walks of life, were to spend a leisurely forty-eight hours from Friday evening to Sunday evening exploring the shallow estuary and rivers at a mere six miles an hour. We tied up or anchored wherever we felt like it to watch the fantastic wildlife; cranes, herons and shags keeping watch on one leg from the branches of river-bank trees, a pack of pelicans toting their picnic hampers along a long narrow sandbank, arrowheads of ducks bisecting the sky, waterfowls flapping triangles of water on the water surfaces, or a school of porpoises (dolphins to some), crabs scuttling on the estuary bottom just a few feet beneath us. Eight of us—with enough food for at least twelve and drink for sixteen, and such marvellous mild weather for mid-winter that anyone from other parts of the world would have thought it either late or early summer. It was even warm enough for some (I most certainly wasn't among them) to throw themselves into the somewhat chilly water—chilly, that is, by Western Australian standards. But most of us preferred to wet ourselves by much less drastic means. Please forgive the levity—I use it deliberately to show just what the atmosphere was: about the least conducive to anything of even the slightest serious content, let alone something like the Christos Experiment.

Even before starting, I felt convinced that we would not be able to proceed far with the one volunteer prepared to subject himself to lying supine for so long, when, after a very good dinner in both quality and quantity, with a great deal of wine on top of the drinks beforehand, he proclaimed himself as incapable, in any case, of maintaining any other position for the next hour or so.

Apart from Leo, who was to massage our experimentee's ankles, and I, who was taking him for the run, there was also David K— in our company, the one who had flown for an hour or so over north Australian landscapes and who wanted to run again if no one else would try it. But for the particular purpose in my mind, I naturally wanted someone who hadn't tried the experiment before, nor even knew much about it. I felt quite sure that we would manage little more than the massaging stage, though I was prepared to find that perhaps some sort of visualization might be accomplished in the early stretching and shrinking exercises.

The experimentee lay on a narrow settee with Leo and I perched at either end. A portable radio was playing Saturday-night pop music and the lights of the houseboat were turned to 'medium' brightness. We had tied up at the riverbank jetty of a country hotel which, as was to be expected on a Saturday night, was providing its own amplified music and fair share of noise. Outside, occasional visitors, curious about the houseboat and its occupants, would make their tentative approaches, although we *had* drawn the curtains to obviate their prying as much as possible. About a hundred yards down-river was a road bridge over which the occasional vehicle roared and clattered. One of our group had gone off to see what greater excitement the hotel might offer and, finding none, reappeared disconcertingly in the middle of the experiment.

This, then, is what happened when the conditions seemed quite unsuitable for accomplishing even the preliminary requisites of the experiment, let alone anything more.

Peter C— is also from another state in Australia as was our previous David B—, but from Victoria this time instead of Queensland, though Victoria is also on the eastern if southern seaboard. He was thirty-two years of age at the time of the experiment and the manager of a restaurant of 'atmosphere'. He has spent some time overseas, especially in Italy, and has his pilot's licence for flying small aircraft, which he does regularly. He is unmarried but has many friends and acquaintances and, as his occupation requires, is a congenial 'professional host', a 'good mixer'. But privately he is an excellent and imaginative host too, and a generous one. He enjoys cooking, especially the rather more exotic dishes he delights in serving to his friends. He is fond of good books, good music and original paintings rather than prints.

Right from the start there was, as I expected, a fair amount of chaffing and laughing and even bawdy comments and suggestions as the massaging began. However, Peter gave himself to the procedure rather better than could be expected and, to my surprise, I found he was soon into the stretching and shrinking exercises, though at first merely with sensation and little if any visualization. But when he said he could indeed see something of his feet and head withdrawing and re-approaching, the others round him gradually became curious and quieter until, contrary to my expectations, I found that the experiment was proceeding as successfully as ever it had.

The memory exercises gave him no problem, even though he automatically selected the front door of his Perth apartment rather than that of any 'home' in Victoria or elsewhere. However, one would naturally expect the visualization-from-the-roof exercise to be especially easy for him as his apartment is on the ninth floor of the building with only one more above it. From both east and west he has superb views of the coastal plain to the Darling Ranges in one direction, and across the river to the city and the lesser hills of Kings Park in the other. On top of this (quite literally as well as imaginatively), he could be expected to be able to visualize from whatever height he managed to attain because he frequently flew in small aircraft. I even expected him, when descending to land, to select and approach an aerodrome as though he were indeed in an aeroplane. Not so.

As had happened with several of us now, he found himself approaching a coast when in actual fact he was some distance from one in either his present physical location in the houseboat or in his location at his apartment. By this time the other observers were awed into complete silence. Someone even turned the radio down a little, not because of its distraction but so that he himself could hear, for Peter's voice had already assumed the quiet but steady monotone I had come to know so well.

The coast where he landed was not at all like any I could recognize from near by in Western Australia; but as he described it minutely it was soon apparent that it was somewhere in Victoria, in a much cooler climate than where we were in actuality, even though it was winter here at the time. The rocky formations and promontories enfolding small beaches that he described were also much more typical of Victorian coastlines than those in Western Australia.

At first he said he was quite alone. There was no one at the beach. It was afternoon, with a few clouds in the sky. He was dressed in some kind of clothing but wasn't sure what it was. Sandals were on his feet, but not any that he possessed now or had before. He thought he was wearing some kind of shirt and shorts, probably green, or perhaps it was a bathing-suit. Then he thought it was indeed a green bathing-suit, but one with a top or one-piece from shoulders to thighs. He thought it was 'old fashioned', but it could be a type of swimming-costume which, for a few, was becoming stylish again.

He was walking along the beach and could see everything in vivid and sharply delineated detail. He kept using the word 'extraordinary'. He thought there were houses somewhere in the neighbourhood, and then was certain that there were but that they weren't visible because of their being beyond the edge of near-by cliffs.

But then he climbed over a small promontory and, as he did so, he described the sea from this higher vantage point, even to a lone fisherman in a boat who was wearing some kind of broad-brimmed hat. The late afternoon sun was shining brilliantly on the sea's stippled surface. Clouds were coloured from deep grey at the centres to gleaming gold at the edges.

Just as he was starting to descend the other side of the promontory to the beach, he could suddenly see people. Yet perhaps even more striking than the presence of people now was a very long line of changing-boxes, standing like sentinel posts, each with its few steps up to its door. Parties of people, in swimming costumes or suitable beach clothes, were sitting around before these changing-boxes, or were swimming in the comparatively calm, almost lagoon-like waters where the lone fisherman was still plying his rod from his boat.

But now he himself was part of one of these groups, and playing with his sister. She was only five years of age and he three. It was not only their own ages which told him that the time he was now in was almost thirty years ago, but the ages of his parents and the clothes worn by everyone around him. He was not particularly 'happy' about being there, though there was nothing about the scene to frighten him. It was more that he was piqued about something, perhaps something he was not allowed to have or do. There was some connection with the changing-boxes, which still stretched in a long straight line as far as the eye could see, rather like a scene in some surrealistic painting.

He and his sister went inside the changing-box where it was naturally darker than outside on the beach, but his eyes soon became accustomed to that. The first thing he saw was an enormous coil of rope, now dry, but tough with salt from the sea. There was also a heap of fishing nets, aged and tangled with disuse.

He and his sister stayed for some time inside the changing-box, happily preoccupied merely with inspecting and playing with the coil of rope and the fishing-net. They might have gone on endlessly, he said, but someone called them to come outside and so they rejoined the family where they sat, still fully-clothed, on the beach.

What followed then was not quite clear, he said. A voice, a male voice, exhorted him to go into the water. He felt sure the voice was not his father's, but he couldn't place whose it might be. All he knew was that he didn't want to go even *near* the water. He was terrified of it. But someone, a male adult, was forcing him towards it, even dragging him. He became more and more terrified and, in actuality, anxiety was plainly visible on his face and tension in his body.

But then, abruptly, he had managed to break away and was running along the beach, away from them all. Away he ran, past the long long line of changing-boxes and towards the point at the end of the beach. Only when he was some distance away did he allow himself to slow down. Then he went and sat up on the promontory, alone, from where he could look down on the lone fisherman in his big hat who was still plying his rod from the small boat anchored out in the bay.

Then he said abruptly that the scene was fading, and then had ended. He sat up and said he was quite 'satisfied' with what he had seen for a first attempt. He didn't think he had been in any previous life, but found it remarkable enough to have been transported back to such early childhood and to an incident which, he now recalled, had actually happened, though he had long since forgotten it.

No, he had not seen anything nearly as vivid as this experience had been, although he dreamt frequently, probably every night. It had all been perfectly logical and, with the one exception of the impossibly long line of changing-boxes which still puzzled him, but which nevertheless he accepted, it had all been as real as, or even more real than, conscious observation in real life.

Despite all the adverse circumstances, it had taken just over an hour altogether when he himself thought it had taken only a quarter of that time. Furthermore, I was not to see Peter again for some six weeks, but he could still remember most details of his experience even then.

This was the tenth experiment with eight different people and two second attempts. In every case at least something had happened, in varying degrees, which was beyond the experience of each one of us. On the other hand, only three of us could say that we had possibly seen a 'past life'—I myself, Ray and Joy. It might be conceded that the two Davids had also glimpsed a past but very recent life which had quite definitely been within the last hundred years compared with the possible several thousand years the first three of us had known. Stephan had been in the present and possibly into a few years in the future. Peter had remained himself, but as a child and at an age of which most would expect to have very little if any memory.

It seemed a very mixed, confused, and confusing bag, except for the one factor of something happening which none of us had experienced before. If for this reason alone, I felt compelled to continue the experiments, and not only to continue but to widen the types of people taken for the run. For it had just occurred to me that there was a gross imbalance in those who, quite haphazardly, had been selected so far—seven men but only the one woman, though ages had ranged from David B—'s twenty-one to my own forty-seven. I decided that the experiment needed to be tried with more women, and also with children and elderly people. I also wanted to try the experiment with someone who, having been blind from birth, has never seen anything at all before. And of course there was still Leo to be tried once more, and Joy to have her second attempt.

But having come about half-way, I should think, through the experiments I wish to make and record, there is one small matter I feel I should comment upon at this stage before proceeding any further—and I realize all too well that I have given much more detail, perhaps even to a tiresomely meticulous degree, in the accounts of my own two experiences than in any other with, perhaps, the one exception of Joy's which was recorded verbatim. It should, of course, be quite obvious that, first of all, as I am so far the only one to record his or her own experience, I am also the only one to know all the details I can possibly record; whereas all the other accounts are merely recordings of what was described to me by the experimentee; moreover, more than probably the experimentee *chose* (in both senses of 'selection' and 'decision') what to relate to me, or perhaps was only able to recount a certain amount to me during the time of the experience. I know all too well just how amazingly much of this detail there *is* to record.

Chapter Thirteen

Richard B–, twenty-four, son of a Dutch father and an English mother, was born in the Netherlands where he stayed for some years before living in both Canada and England and now in Australia. He is a male nurse and at the present time is working in a large old men's home. He is knowledgeable about antiques, rare books and prints and old silver, and collects what he can with his restricted financial resources. He buys attractive pieces of old furniture and repairs them himself, removing polish or paint from the wood and then waxing the surfaces to show the beauty of the grain and of the pieces of furniture themselves which he keeps for his own use.

In the world's present 'permissive' society, he said—after the experiment—he is bisexual, and has no 'hang-ups' over sexuality, choosing his partners from either sex for their personality and physical beauty, their essential 'ingredients' being in that order. He is quietly well-spoken with an English accent that would be considered in that country as 'upper middle class'. He hadn't heard of this experiment but came to my apartment with David K– and, when the subject cropped up, consented to try a run himself, though he said afterwards that at the time he had been quite convinced that nothing would 'happen'. I was particularly interested in the opportunity to try him as I found that before his arrival in Australia he had taken two 'trips' on LSD; he was, therefore, my first experimentee who could make a comparison of both experiences.

The run was tape-recorded, Leo massaging his ankles and I his forehead. It was a wild winter night with gale-force winds, though these can barely be heard from inside my 'noise-proofed' apartment.

David K– was a silent observer of the entire session.

Richard chose to lie on the carpet with two large cushions under his head and another on either side of his bare feet, 'to support them without strain', having removed socks as well as shoes. There was no accompanying music so that occasional external sounds could be heard now and again – a car hooting, people on the stairs outside my door, the occupants above arriving home and making barely audible yet still detectable noises.

After the preliminary massaging, which he found 'pleasant but not at all confusing', he accomplished the visualized stretching, shrinking and expanding exercises with remarkable ease. He also described his front door with great detail, even down to scratches left from having to break in with a jemmy when he had once locked himself out; however, he chose the door of the place where he had been living for some time before moving into a new flat only two nights prior to the experiment. Almost immediately upon being required to give descriptions, his eyelids flickered rapidly and it was quite easy to see his eyes moving underneath the closed lids, these eye and eyelid movements recurring frequently during the run.

His descriptions from the top of the roof were also surprisingly detailed, even to the clouds of a 'dull afternoon'. However, he had difficulty with ascending and had to make three attempts, twice having quickly descended almost back to the rooftop. The sky, he said, had become totally overcast, although there was neither wind nor rain.

When I asked him to attempt going up *through* the cloud, he almost immediately did so with ease, describing the cold and damp sensation of being completely 'fogged in' by the cloud, 'like a clammy cream'. When he 'broke through', he was almost dazzled by the brightness of the blue sky above and the beauty of the undulating carpet of clouds beneath him.

After a while, I asked him if he could see *through* these clouds somewhere and, if so, could he distinguish land or water or anything at all below. He said there was no break in the clouds, but he could 'make one' just as previously he agreed that he himself had changed day to night and back to day again, the night being one of calmness and bright moonlight over a lake (one that existed in the district where he had until recently lived).

I therefore asked him to make his own break in the clouds

and he immediately saw land far below. There was little if any habitation and it seemed dark and bleak with low shrubs. Water glinted here and there. As he descended through the clouds, the landscape below became shaded and dull again.

From now on he was tape-recorded, his voice soon assuming the quiet monotone now so familiar in the experiment. At times he was obviously so absorbed that he made no attempt to give any description, and even seemed to resent prompting from me to find out what he was seeing.

He landed on 'soft black ground' with very green grass and puddles of water here and there. Then he realized that he was on the edge of a marsh, or at least marshy ground. He could see 'plants with sticks with brown ends—what were they called? Ah yes, bulrushes.' The ground was 'a bit soft' although it was quite firm where he was standing. He was not at all apprehensive about being caught in boggy ground, let alone quicksands, as he was already walking towards higher and higher ground.

He could see his feet very clearly. They were quite bare and rather pink, the same size as they were in reality, although normally they were not pink at all. He was wearing a pair of brown trousers, when in actuality his trousers were maroon. His visualized trousers had wide legs while his actual ones were rather tight.

But now, when he again looked at his feet, he found that he was wearing a pair of leather sandals, with leather straps intertwining around his legs almost up to his knees. As his eyes followed them up his legs, his trousers seemed either to shrink or disappear till he was, he said, now wearing some kind of tunic, again made of leather, but of strips with alternating lengths, the end of each strip being scalloped in a semi-circle.

He was now walking quite steadily along a narrow and worn path ascending a hill, but with the hill falling away sharply on either side so that it was more like a wall with the path 'sunk' about eighteen inches. The path, made of 'dirt', was very dry and quite unmade. He was alone; but other people must use the path frequently, he said, as it was very worn. There was no sign of habitation, but he knew habitation to be not far away as that was where he was going.

His surroundings were rather desolate and rocky. He had not been there before and it was quite unfamiliar to him. There were hills in the distance, very sharply etched, with some quite dead-looking trees, like trees in a winter landscape although there was no snow. They were 'very low and very wide, touching each other so that there is a whole line of trees, but they have no foliage at all, just branches'. He thought he had seen this kind of tree somewhere before, but he couldn't remember where.

He was still alone. When asked if he thought there might be somebody else, somewhere, he said 'not yet'. I asked him to look at his hands and see if he was wearing anything on them. He said he was wearing a largish ring on his right hand, when in actuality he was wearing a signet ring of conventional size on the third finger of his right hand. The visualized ring had a pearl set in a disc or circle of gold from which there were carved lions all the way round the ring.

He was now wearing a breastplate, 'some kind of Roman costume, with red, lots of red, and silver, everything silver and red'. He also had a plumed helmet, the plume being stiff, 'fairly solid', and again red. He was carrying a shield and a spear. The shield, emblazoned with a golden eagle, he carried in his left hand with his forearm passing through a leather strap, or hasp, until his hand could reach and grip a second one. The spear was about five feet long and made of metal with a dark shaft and a 'yellowy' or golden arrowhead.

But he had now moved on and could see a wall and archway, towards which he was walking. The path was widening out into almost a road, yet was still not paved or sealed in any way, until it reached the pillars on either side of the arch, through which he was now passing.

He could now see many stone buildings and the inner side of the wall. Here there were carpets hanging—carpets patterned in dark red and orange squares with small orange lines proceeding from one square into another. He had never seen this kind of carpet before. There were six of them altogether, but he had already passed them and was entering the building area, proceeding down a long, arched and pillared corridor or colonnade.

He was among people now, but not traffic. People were all round him; and the place—a market, he could now see—was very busy. There were men, women and children; a group of women all in black, like nuns, were carrying food. There were a lot of stalls in this colonnade under its arched ceiling, where all sorts of food and fruit and vegetables were sold. But these were not what he had come for.

When asked in which part of the world he thought he was, he immediately answered, 'It seems like some part under Roman domination, I think somewhere between the English and Scottish border.' In any case, he was quite sure it was in Britain during the time of the Roman occupation.

He himself was a Roman, he said, and here and there were Romans dressed identically to himself. They were soldiers. Other people wore very loose and colourful clothes, and these were *not* Romans. Their clothes did not at all consist of trousers and shirts, but were more 'toga-like', mostly to the ground and 'wrapped' around them. It was a fairly civilized place. The Romans, at least, did shave. He himself was not living there; he was stationed there, for only a short while so far, he didn't know how long exactly.

He was not what he would call happy there, but was quite content. At present he was 'amusing' himself. When asked if he had parents or family, he said, 'It doesn't worry me. No, but it doesn't worry me.' He wasn't at all homesick for any particular place or people. He took life as it came, enjoying himself wherever he happened to be. When asked a few more questions of this kind, he brushed them off almost impatiently with, 'I'm going in through one of the doors very shortly.' It was 'pretty dark' beyond the double doors with a sign overhead denoting what the building was, and he 'knew' he had come to this town to go into that building—a bath-house.

There were a lot of people inside and he heard sounds of many voices as he left his shield and spear, armour and helmet at a booth for this purpose just inside the building, which was partly open-roofed and partly closed in. The people were both men and women, but there were no children now. Children were not allowed in this particular bath-house because it was also a 'pleasure-house'.

Most of the people were in the two square pools with the water coming up to their shoulders. They were playing quite unashamedly with each other, men with women, men with men or women with women, it didn't matter. People came here to do or 'have' what they wanted. Some were walking around either completely naked or, as he himself was, with only a rather skimpy piece of some kind of fabric around their loins.

He had now moved away from the square with these open-air pools to go to another 'room' with curtained-off cubicles on either side. He was looking into these cubicles 'to see what he would have'. Then he made up his mind and entered one of the cubicles.

At this point he said hardly anything for quite some time; and when he did, it was only after several promptings. When asked to tell what he was doing, he said, 'I don't think I should; it will be awfully depraved. It is more of a brothel than a bath-house.'

When prompted further, he was again impatient but did say that he was looking into other cubicles to see what he would have, woman or man, girl or boy, it didn't matter which, and no one took any notice of whatever one did. They didn't even *look*, as they were too busy themselves, either in couples or 'groups playing games—sexual games'.

He didn't recognize anyone else there, but he focused for a while on two old men, 'very old', who were 'having things done to them', he wouldn't say what. Indeed, he now said that he could stop the experiment at this point if he wanted to, but he didn't at all want to, he was so absorbed in it and wanted to 'see' what he himself was going to do even though he really felt he already knew.

He was now in a section where there were no longer women and girls, and he was still looking. Then he found he had chosen a cubicle with a settee in it, and only the one boy, whereas several of the cubicles would have more than one boy or man, 'depending on what one wanted'. He didn't have to pay, not now. Nor had he paid anything when he had entered and left his armour and so forth at the booth. 'You pay when you leave, depending on what you have had.'

The cubicle was built of stone. The walls were decorated and the settee was of beautifully carved marble. Yet the floor was wooden.

He had now decided to take this cubicle with the beautiful youth who was enticing him. He particularly liked this youth for his good build, his dark curly hair, the hair on his body and, more especially, his 'beautiful smile'.

They did not speak to each other. Should they do so, he was not sure that they could understand each other. In any case it wasn't at all necessary to speak; they had mutual and instant attraction for each other, both becoming almost immediately physically excited. He lay supine on the marble couch with the youth kneeling between his legs. He could now feel the youth's caresses and dexterous ministrations.

From this point it took some coaxing before he would relate what was happening, and now I am not sure whether the next sequence of events would have occurred of its own accord or whether it was due to my persistent plying of questions to know what was happening, for this was the first experience of any sexual intercourse or even 'play' from any of the experiments. To explain the following dialogue between Richard and me: the youth was performing fellatio on Richard, the Roman soldier—but the Richard in the present, on my apartment floor, was feeling no signs of sexual excitement whatsoever as his possible former self participated in highly erotic acts. Furthermore, he acknowledged being perfectly aware of both 'past' and present. Our tape-recorded dialogue—which I decided not to use verbatim as it was much too desultory and would take three to four times the page-space to recount—was as follows:

G. You don't speak at all?

R. There is no need to speak.

G. No? You don't know his name?

R. No.

G. Or if you'll see him again?

R. No.

G. Or is it something that just happens, and when it's over, it's over? Is that it?

R. Well, I *think* it's that.

G. Does he have a name at all? (Pause) Do *you* have a name? (Pause) There is no curiosity from either of you to know who the other is? (Pause) He knows you are a Roman? (Pause) Maybe not, because you have only that one piece of clothing on?

R. He just *works* here, Gerry.

G. And he doesn't take any notice?

R. No.

G. And you are quite content with being there?

R. Yes.

G. You are enjoying it?

R. Oh, yes!

G. Do you know your own name?

R. There is a name that keeps coming up, but I don't know whether it is my own name. And when you say, 'Do you know your name?', I think of a name but I don't know whether it is mine.

G. That doesn't matter. What is the name you are thinking of?

R. Trimalchio.

G. Tri-mal-chio? Have you heard it before?

R. Perhaps.

G. Can you write it? Do you know how to write this name?

R. Yes. T-R-I-M-A-L-C-H-I-O.

G. It's a Latin name? And you see the normal Latin alphabet? Not the Greek alphabet, or anything like that?

R. No.

He would hardly reply to any more questions but would merely frown and slightly shake his head with irritation until some time later on when:

G. Do you *feel* anything for him?

R. It is purely physical.

G. Do you have any love affairs?—say, you are away from somebody or—

R. (Interjecting) Not at the moment.

G. You have had, or not?

R. Yes.

G. Do you know with whom it was? (Pause) Another man? A woman? Are you married?

R. Not married, and no children.

G. Who was it you had a love-affair with?

R. Another man.

G. What happened? (Pause) Is that finished? Or are you separated? Or what?

R. Separated.

G. Do you know where he is?

R. Somewhere else.

G. He isn't just back in Italy, or Rome? Just somewhere else?

R. Yes.

G. You are both posted to two different places?

R. Yes.

G. Was it deliberately done for that, or is it just one of these accidents that happen?

R. Just an accident.

G. Do you expect to see him again?

R. Perhaps.

G. Do you *want* to see him again?

R. Yes.

G. But you don't know if you *do* see him again? (Pause) Do you know his name?

R. No, but I can see him.

He was blond, a couple of years older, and a soldier of the same rank. Did R. have a memento of him? A ring, the one he was wearing and had spoken about before, the one with the gold and the pearl and the lions. He himself had given his lover a bracelet which he wore on his right wrist. While it lasted, he said, it had been a very happy relationship, 'the only one that matters'.

I then decided to throw in what was possibly the most distracting kind of question of all: 'Are you aware that we are now on three different levels, shall we say? You are in the cubicle with the boy, but thinking of your "friend" somewhere else, and you are also here on the floor?'

The reply came back too promptly for him even to have had time to think about it: 'Yes.'

I then asked him if he had anything more he wanted to say about the situation, but he said he had lost interest. I expected him to open his eyes and so finish the experiment, but he went on to say that the boy with him in the cubicle was now most unhappy because he had failed to bring him, Richard, to 'satisfaction'. He was trying to comfort the boy by putting an arm round his shoulder but they still did not speak; he felt sure now that they would not understand each other even if they did speak. The boy was still most unhappy and he himself felt sad, and regretful about the 'futility' of the whole business.

And then the experience was finished. He opened his eyes and sat up.

I was going to let him rest a while, particularly as I was rather tired myself with this run, which had taken well over an hour, though Richard thought it had been merely twenty minutes or so. It was then he said that previously he had been quite convinced that nothing would happen. But now he not only found this far more realistic and meaningful than either of the two trips he had experienced with LSD, when he had merely 'seen' music in the form of colours—music appearing, growing, and disappearing like soap-bubbles from a Technicolour bubble-pipe—and walls which had wavered and rippled like silk in the wind.

He was quite convinced that he had indeed experienced some kind of a return to a past life; his personality, he said, had been much the same then as it was now, though his physical appearance had been very different. He also said it was quite clear to him that this past life he had seen had shown him, as plainly as anything could show him, just how futile and meaningless was a life of casual affairs, let alone promiscuity. It made him feel determined to seek just as soon as he could some 'meaningful relationship' with man or woman, girl or boy—it didn't matter to him just as long as the relationship was meaningful.

He said that he would like to try the experiment again, even several times, but that he would rather leave it for a while until he had time to 'sort out his life a little'. Perhaps, it occurred to me, he had already done this just prior to the experiment, when he had moved from living in a huge old rented barn of a building, which had once been a municipal hall and chambers, into sharing a spacious modern flat with magnificent harbour views. Also, his parents had just left to return to Canada and, he said, he now felt entirely free to lead a completely new life.

Chapter Fourteen

An evening was at last found for Joy's second turn. As was only to be expected, she accomplished the stretching and visualization exercises much more easily and quickly than on her first attempt, and then the memory-visualization exercises from before her front door and from up on her roof. These done, she ascended quickly towards the sky—almost impatiently, I thought—giving quite graphic descriptions of the changing to night from daytime and then back again before ascending further into and above the fleecy sunlit clouds she could 'see' at night from her living-room floor. After a short while I asked her to come down through the clouds and she did so. Then I made sure that she could see land somewhere accessible and she descended towards it in 'brilliant sunshine'.

Once more our original four were present, though Ray chose to see to the dishes in the kitchen while the trip was in progress as Leo, after massaging Joy's ankles, was tape-recording the run. It was a calm, mild night in late winter which, in this particular year of 1971 in Western Australia, was really bland enough to be spring already.

Repeating the tape-recording always takes much more space than if I merely recount the experiment, but once more this second run of Joy's was so graphic and full of interesting and indeed fantastic detail that I have decided to present the entire recording.

The experiment took less than an hour, so I do not think that she had time to concoct it all, or even any of it, as she went along—though after a while I must admit that, as I had also done at one stage with Richard's 'Roman' experience, I became a little suspicious that perhaps she might be 'having me on', or at least making up some of it. But on listening to her rapid, even excited speech afterwards—and her complete lack of hesitation which, rather, was most of the time impatient interjection on her part—I had to admit that it all seemed quite genuine. And I had come to this conclusion even before I confronted her with my previous suspicions when she immediately protested, in a calm and even slightly puzzled manner, as though she was incredulous at the notion even occurring to me.

I have also repeated some of the conversation—at times with all four of us—which ensued after she had 'returned'; yet not *all* of it, as after a while it was only repetition, almost complete repetition, of most of the details and much of the conversation with other people she had seen on the trip.

However, it has just occurred to me that there is at least one extra advantage in presenting the tape-recording verbatim, with no editing, and that is to show how, when running an experimentee, I try not to use questions which might be suggestible. Not only this, but a good deal of the character of an experimentee naturally comes through from the speech mannerisms and expressions used, even though these naturally enough consist of a good deal of remote Western Australia's colloquialisms.

But here now is Joy's second run:

J. I'm coming down to a bay.

G. *Into* a bay, or *towards* a bay?

J. Towards a bay.

G. Can you see the piece of ground you're going to land on?

J. Yes.

G. Is it sand or rock?

J. With rocks around it. It's a shallow bay. The water is very beautiful and clean. I've landed.

G. You've landed? What are you standing on?

J. Sand.

G. Can you see anything else around you?

J. Rocks.

G. Just rocks?

J. Yellowish-brown rocks.

G. Are you walking, or just standing looking around?

J. I'm just looking around—I seem to be covered in sand.

G. Oh! You can see your feet?

J. I have no shoes on.

G. You have bare feet? Anything else about your feet at all?

J. They are biggish feet—long feet—and long and thin legs.

G. Can you see any clothes as yet?

J. No.

G. No clothing yet. Do you think you have any clothes on? Or none at all?

J. I don't have a *feeling* of clothes about me. I notice my feet are very long, big toes, very sinewy. I'm crunching on the sand, looking at my feet. They're awfully *big* feet!

G. Are they surprisingly big?

J. Surprisingly big! I guess about size eight. Too big for a woman. And that ugly toenail!

G. *Are* you a woman?

J. I don't know.

G. What is around you?

J. Rocks.

G. Just rocks?

J. I'm going to climb a rock now.

G. You're climbing a rock. Are there any birds or animals around you?

J. I see a few birds.

G. What kind of birds?

J. Seagulls.

G. Do they see you?

J. They seem to look around, but I think they're used to people being around, because they're not surprised at my presence.

G. Is it easy to get on the rock, or difficult?

J. Quite easy, I've long arms and hands. I'm now viewing myself from the back of me. I have long hair—long beige hair to my shoulders. Fine hair. I've got a band around my head and I've got a staff in my hand—a crooked staff. I'm on top of the rock and I'm looking around with my hand over my eye. And I see water, the bay, and a bird.

G. Any habitation?

J. Very little.

G. Are there any people?

J. Not at this moment.

G. Any animals?

J. No.

G. Can you see what you are wearing now? (Pause) Can you

see the band around your head? (Pause) Your long hair? (Pause) You're carrying a staff? Is it heavy?

J. Quite light.

G. What length is it?

J. About four feet—five feet—something like that.

G. What's it made of?

J. Not sure. It's fine. Very fine—

G. Metal or wood?

J. It seems to be metal. And it's got a little strap at the top of it, and I've got that wrapped around my left wrist. I'm looking at my hands—and they are long, very long hands. Long bony wrists. I'm very flat-chested, skinny. Extremely skinny. I've got full lips, and big beige eyelashes. Largish nose. Fine skin.

G. And you've got a leather strap around your left wrist?

J. A leather strap around the left wrist.

G. Anything else about it? Do you know what you use it for?

J. No.

G. Can you see any clothes yet?

J. I'm wearing a wide, loose, white garment—a very simple garment with a cord around the waist. A simple neckline and sleeves half-way down with a kind of finish in gold and grey. It's not very ornate.

G. Have you ever possessed a garment like that?

J. It seems to be something I'm wearing all the time.

G. I mean have you one like that *now* in your possession?

J. No.

G. No? It is only what you are wearing *there*?

J. Yes.

G. Is there anything else? You have no form of shoes? You are still in bare feet?

J. Absolutely in bare feet. But the sensation I have is of absolute sure-footedness as I walk along these rocks now. And I am looking towards solid ground. And I feel that the sand is sort of easy under my feet, the hard rocks don't seem to disturb the feeling under my feet. I don't flinch at the harshness of the rocks. I'm evidently not used to wearing shoes. I've *hardened* feet.

G. But do you feel the sand?

J. Oh, yes. I can feel the warmth of the sand and the crunch of the rock. My right toenail *is* dirty! Quite dirty! It's as though something is in it, but it doesn't bother me. I feel as though I should clean it, but I think 'Oh, bother!' I'm thirsty. I want to go to find a well.

G. Do you know which way to walk for water?

J. Yes. I'm facing east. I'm going east. There is a little path away from the rocks—I'm taking that now—with bushes, and it's not very high. I'm coming to whiter rocks, white sandstone. There are several sections of the rock obviously made by men to walk farther down beyond this place. I'm coming down and I'm using my hand—I've put my staff into my right hand and I'm crunching back and assisting myself in a backward sense on to the lower ground. I've reached it. And I'm looking around, dusting the rock off my hand. I think I have to hurry for some reason.

G. Do you know where you are hurrying to?

J. It is a long track, sandy and dry. Beautiful clear day. I'm pushing through the bushes on the left. There are two sheep on the left. Two sheep.

G. Are they the same size?

J. Lovely—the same size. Exactly six months old. Little sheep. They look up at me and they are disturbed.

G. Are they white?

J. Grey. They are not white. They've been recently shorn.

G. Are there any other sheep nearby?

J. Not that I can see. There are all sorts of trees.

G. Do you know what kind of trees?

J. No, with a fine leaf. And they are very tall. (Author's note: tamarisks, perhaps? Or cypresses?)

G. Is it a leaf that hangs down?

J. No. It is a bushy type of tree, and gives an awful lot of shade. I'm going past the trees, down to a lower hill. The sun is intensely fierce.

G. You're quite hot? Do you get sunburned at all?

J. Very hot, yeah. But it doesn't seem to bother me.

G. You haven't come to a place to drink yet?

J. Yes. I'm coming now to a shed.

G. What is it made of?

J. Wood and bark. Wood base and bark top.

G. Doesn't it have doors and windows?

J. Just a door and an open window. And I'm going inside.

G. Are you inside?

J. Yes, I'm inside.

G. What can you see?

J. A rough bed with a blanket on it. A rough table, a bench, a trough made of wood. And the trough has got water in it. Cool water. There is a jar on the table, which is roughly made. I pick up the jar and I go and scoop the water out of the trough and I have a lovely cold drink. Then I wipe the heat from my brow with a rag I have just removed from the side of the open window.

G. What colour rag?

J. White.

G. What kind of material?

J. Cotton, very rough.

G. Can you see the bed again? Are there blankets on it? What kind of blankets? And what colour?

J. Spun blankets, hand-spun. And it (*sic*) is red and green, blue and grey, and brown. Woven in pyramid designs.

G. And the bed itself, is it a wooden bed?

J. It's got two wooden slings with animal skins slung between them and stitched coarsely on either side to the pole. And I have a little pallet like a pillow, very soft. And this is where I sleep. It is my little hut.

G. This is where you are. You are all alone?

J. Yes. But I'm quite happy to be alone. And—I'm a man! I'm a *man* now and *not* a woman! Because I feel I want to relieve myself and I have a man's genitals. They are very thin and long and skinny like me. There is a donkey outside the door. He is my pet. He is eating the little plants out of the pot I have in the window. I'm a simple soul. I like simple things. I'm quite happy in this element.

G. Do you have a name?

J. There is no name in my mind at the moment.

G. Can you tell me roughly how old you are?

J. I'm about thirty-five.

G. Do you have a beard or not?

J. No. I've got thick lips and bushy eyebrows and a sandy complexion. I've got this thing over my head that I haven't noticed—a white cloth with a leather type of thing that is holding the cloth on my head. I think I'm hungry and I am going to get myself something to eat. I go to a little shelf and a little cupboard. I have made this cupboard myself.

G. Of what kind of wood?

J. Rough—rough planks of wood. I'm opening the cupboard and inside it on the shelf there is a big lump of bread and it's got bumps and holes but it is very tasty and I can't wait to get at that bread. And there is a jar of goat's milk. And I'm going to sit down and have my jar of milk and that bread. I know there is a vine at the back and I think I will go to get these grapes and wash them and that is what I really am looking forward to. I'm going outside now and walk around the donkey that is standing there quite happily. He has a thick coat of hair and is eating my daisies. And I let it because he has had them anyway. And I am so fond of that donkey, he is really a great friend. He has a look at me as though he's saying, 'Ha, ha! You're home now! Where the heck have you been all day?' There are not a lot of grapes there; only a few bunches are left.

G. What colour grapes?

J. Purple grapes.

G. Can you see what the shed is made of?

J. It is made of bark and old planks and half-rounded trunks. It is very small; it is about ten feet by eight. It is very tiny. There is a tree outside that shelters it from the very fierce sun. But I love this place; it is comfortable and it is simple and it's mine.

G. What time of the year is it?

J. It's summer.

G. Where do you think it is? Which part of the world do you think it is?

J. In the Middle East. Definitely. There is a lot of water around. There is a well. There is a well a little farther away. And I know where that well is. It's a simple stone well.

G. Did you dig it yourself?

J. No, I think it has been provided by whoever was here before. But I go there every day and get the water. I'm sitting down and eating my bread and enjoying the grapes. The donkey looks as though he is hungry and I get up and break off a bit of the bread and give it to the donkey.

G. There is a donkey and there is a goat too?

J. There is a goat somewhere because I'm drinking goats' milk. I just know it's goats' milk. It is somewhere around.

G. Do you know the name of the donkey yet?

J. No. The only name that comes to my mind is Mooka, or something like that.

G. Mooka?

J. Mooka.

G. Do you think *you* have a name yet?

J. My name is Yahbi.

G. Yahbi?

J. Yahbi.

G. How do you spell it?

J. I don't know. I know I'm called Yahbi. I'm Yahbi.

G. Do you have any family at all?

J. There doesn't seem to be.

G. Do you remember ever having had parents? Or some kind of family?

J. I have an old mother somewhere tucked away. She is at some distance. I have chosen to live like this because I didn't want her to interfere in my life. And I know I have a simple life here.

G. How do you live?

J. I think I look after people's sheep. That's all I can think of.

G. Can you see what you are wearing?

J. I have no shoes on, and a simple white garment, and very simple things. But I'm a very happy person in myself. I've got very spiritual ideas about life, and I just don't want to be associated with masses of people. It's my own kind of religion. And I think it is in the time *after* Christ. And I just feel that being by myself and doing the simple things and living a pure life, which is *very* pure, I'm happy!

G. Is there much of a change in climate? Do you have to store food?

J. It doesn't appear so. It seems to be long, hot and dry; a monotonous dull climate with lots of clear sky.

G. Is there any other fruit on the trees?

J. There seem to be oranges on the trees along the road, where I know they are. (Meaning the oranges.)

G. There is a road?

J. There is that road which goes right past my little hut.

G. And what kind of a road is it?

J. Well worn, by me and my sheep and my donkey and perhaps by other people. And I know I go down past the tall tree and get on to another hill. And there in the valley amongst the little hills is a small village. *Round* is the village. The roofs are all round and white. There is a wall around the city. And I am about a hundred yards from the gate and I have my donkey with me. I'm not riding it, I'm just holding it with its leash. And on the side of the donkey I have some provisions in a white sack, I don't know what it is, I think they're pumpkins. Or some sort of produce that I've got in there. I think I go to do some trading, that's what I've come here for. That's where I instinctively go. I am going into the gate and it's all sunlight and there are lots of women and children about.

G. What is the gate?

J. A big metal gate and simple structures with spikes on them. The people are streaming in and out and there are chooks (fowls) and goats and kids all about the gate and inside the wall. Houses with white, raised courtyards and windows and doors. I'm going into one of these places because that one's courtyard is the market-place. I have made up my mind and I'm going there. Nobody takes notice of me.

G. Nobody takes notice of you?

J. No. They all go happily about.

G. What kind of people are they? White or brown?

J. They are Arabian, not white people.

G. They are not as fair as you?

J. They are not as fair as me, no. The women are short and dumpy and have olive complexions and brown eyes. They carry their babies on their backs. And they have got simple garments and they have pots on their heads, some of them. Very simple people.

G. Do you know the name of the village at all?

J. No. I'm looking around to try to discover if the village has a name. It doesn't seem to have a name. But I'm going to see a man called Krala. That's the man I've got to see.

G. Do you know why you've got to see him?

J. It has something to do with the market-place. I see him now. Here he is; he is there. He has evidently been waiting for me. A man with a beard and fiery eyes. A kind man, taller than me. He is an Arab, very skinny. He says, 'Ah, Yahbi! You've come to see me. Where have you been?' And I say to him, 'I haven't had to come in for any provisions lately.' He says to me, 'We've missed you.' And I say, 'Why?' And he says, 'Oh, you're so good to the children.'

G. Which children?

J. The children of the city. Evidently they love me. I tell them stories. Beautiful stories. 'Come over here, and sit down,' he is saying to me now. So I go over and leave my donkey and tie him to a branch of a little tree against the wall of the village. And it is still very hot and sunny. We sit down and he brings out a kind of cheese and asks me if I would like a piece and I say, 'Yes, I'll have a piece.' He cuts off a piece with a big knife with a rough-boned handle. And I take it and he knows it is a treat for me and I say, 'I wish I could take some of it home.' And he says, 'Yahbi, you can take this home, I'll give it to you.' And I'm very pleased because that is for me a great treat. And I know he can afford it, he is quite well off this man; he is a merchant. I'm going to ask him what happens here today. 'There is a meeting. There is a man coming to talk to them.' 'Ah, what kind of a man is he?' I want to know. 'He is a leader of men,' he says. 'What does he look like?' 'They call him the Great One,' he says. 'Can I listen to him?' 'Anyone can listen to him,' he says. 'When is he coming?' I want to know. He says, 'He will be here shortly. He comes to talk to the people.' He seems to be excited about it.

I ask Krala to tell me about this man. 'I don't know anything about him; I only know what the people say. And they say he's a very good and wonderful person. And he's going to talk to the people today. He has travelled many miles.' 'And how old is he?' I say. 'About twenty-three.' 'Twenty-three? How is he so wise when he is only twenty-three?' And I'm repeating this in front of Krala because this is what comes to my mind. And he says, 'Ah, sometimes young heads have wise thoughts.' And I'm puzzled at that one. I'm not very clever. I keep asking him why is *he* so clever? And he says, 'Now Yahbi, you be patient.' 'Oh, I think I'd better not speak any more.'

Then a woman is coming over and on her back is a little baby, tied round with an old towel. She has a sweet face. 'Why don't you come and see us, Yahbi?' she says. 'You never call and see us.' And I say, 'I don't like to impose.' 'Ah Yahbi, you tell my children such beautiful stories. Why don't you come? They long to hear your stories.' I think of the few pumpkins I have to sell and I go to the donkey and take the pumpkins out of the white bag. This is part of their (the people's) diet. They are lovely pumpkins. And she says, 'Will you cut off some for me, Yahbi? I will pay you some money for it.' And I get my knife I've got tied in my belt, somewhat similar to Krala's knife, and I cut a piece off for her and say, 'This is my present to you, I don't want any money.' And she says, 'Ah Yahbi, you're so good. You're a good man, Yahbi.' At that moment there is a ruffle; people are all getting excited. Somebody is coming through the gate on a donkey. (Pause).

G. What are you doing?

J. I'm staring with my mouth open. The man on the donkey is Jesus. And he has the most beautiful eyes. And I am at once aware of my own inadequacy. He looks at me. He looks at all the people. There is a greatness about him that is indescribable. Not something I can describe. He is wearing a simple white garment and it comes to my mind he is dressed identically like me. He gets off the donkey. And he goes to wash his feet in a trough by the side of the road. A woman comes and gives him a towel to wipe them. He thanks her and someone comes forward with a pitcher of water for him to drink from and he drinks. Except for his eyes he looks exactly like everybody else. I don't know him as I know him *now*, if you know what I mean. His name is Jesus, but I don't know a thing about him. Except that he is a great teacher and everyone is going to hear him for the first time.

Quietly he gets himself down on the concrete (?) side of a well in the courtyard. It is about one foot from the ground. It is like a platform and he goes to sit on the side of the well. And he puts his hands in his lap and he is addressing them as 'My children' and he is saying, 'I came to tell you of the great things which are in store for all mankind.' I'm not frightened by him but I am bewildered. I feel that he is going to have some influence on my life and I don't know what it is and the feeling is that I have to change my life for him from that of a simple man that attends (*sic*) the goats. And I don't want to give up that life because it is so easy, it is so simple, so—compact. And I feel in the bottom of my body he is going to ask me to give it up.

I'm beginning to be a bit resentful of him now. I'm going to turn away from him now because I don't want to be called by him for some reason. I have a deep knowledge that he is going to call me to help him in some way and I don't like the thought. So I turn to the other man I was talking to and tell him I'm going inside out of the sun. 'Aren't you going to listen?' he says. And I say, 'No, I've had enough of his talk. You can tell me afterwards what he said. I'll see you later at the square.' 'All right,' Krala says. 'Don't forget to take your cheese.' I nearly forgot. 'I'll come later to sell the pumpkins, after the sun is down.' 'You can leave them inside my door,' he says. And I take the bag and go over to his dwelling which is the inner part of a room in a little hut made of white stone, similar to all the others. And I place them inside this door.

I go into this hut because I have been here many times. Not really a hut—it is a dwelling. It is very cool and the ceiling is not low and it has a dirt floor. There are wooden rafters of some kind. They have nice stools and tables and they have been scrubbed clean white. This place is a lot more comfortable than my place; after all, he is a merchant. There are some steps leading up to some sleeping quarters. I've never been up there and I want to investigate (*sic*) my curiosity. I've never been invited to look. I think, 'Hah! Now is the time to look, when nobody is here.' So I go upstairs and pass the little mid-balcony and then I see four simple white beds, much the same as mine but better finished. Simple white towels are all folded neatly on the end of the bed. And this is where I know he and his wife and their two children sleep. I know he's got two children, two boys, they are about sixteen. I come down the steps. I have satisfied my curiosity. And I leave the pumpkins on the inside of the door and I walk out. I turn back to see this man Jesus, with his hands uplifted, talking to the people. But he's got his back to me and I think instinctively, 'I won't bother to go and listen to him. Blow him! I'll go elsewhere and have a lie down, I'm feeling tired.' Because I know if I go back there, somehow or other he's going to get me to do something or other for him and I don't want to change my way of thinking or—and this is something I *know*—if I move back there I'll *do* this. So I go outside the wall. And outside the wall I sit in the shade. And I take the cheese out of my pocket and I relish each mouthful. My curiosity about the man is considerable, but I just feel I want to leave it there. I just want to leave it there, I don't want to pursue it any further. I look down at my dirty toenail; I really am a bit sloppy! I know if I go inside I've got to pass that man, for that's where my donkey is. So I'll stay outside here till the talk has finished. I'm falling asleep. I'm tired. I want to sleep. (Pause.)

G. Have you gone to sleep then? Or are you back?

J. I'm back.

G. What do you think happened then? Or don't you think anything happened?

J. I just think I went to sleep. I was tired. It was so vivid again, you know.

G. Was it daytime all the time?

J. Daytime *all* the time. I knew when I got outside that wall, it was sort of my way of protecting myself from that man, you know? I just had a deep feeling of knowingness in the bottom of my body here, when he looked at me with his fantastic eyes. He had a simple face. He was tall. Not terribly tall, but thin, as most of the men seemed to be. And the women seemed to be fattish, very Arabian in features. Jewish, Arabian. And round and squat. Rather *un*beautiful. Thick eyebrows but beautiful eyes. But he had that sort of a—he didn't have the look we see in paintings of Jesus, but I just knew he was Jesus, because he was the man they said who was coming. I didn't know anything about him at all, you know. He was a man coming, called Jesus, and he was a great talker. A speaker. And a holy person. That's all that preceded him to the village the day I got there.

I was a terribly simple person, almost naïve. I was completely untutored. I couldn't spell. But there was a sort of happiness, a purity, about me. A *goodness* about me. A 'good soul', you know. I was happy with my donkey, I loved my goats, and I seemed to love the sheep and I loved my simple little dwelling. I was very tall and skinny, but fair. Pale skin, the same as mine. My hands were long and bony. My hair was fine, soft, and beige. I was a bit untidy, a bit sloppy, but clean. And I was perfectly happy knowing I was going to my little hut...

The bread was round. It wasn't flat, it was sort of roundish and there were seeds of some kind in it. I don't know where I got the bread. Maybe I made it. It seemed that I evidently lived on the grapes, the milk, and there was honey there. I know because there was a jar with some of the creamed honey in it. I drank a lot of water and I was enormously healthy.

G. You didn't eat meat?

J. I didn't appear to eat meat. I do know that when I walked into my little hut I was very pleased and a great feeling of inner happiness was within me. I was unlettered and uneducated; I couldn't read or write. My animals loved me and I had an affinity with children and I evidently told beautiful stories to children. And the village children loved me because I used to talk to them and weave wonderful tales for them. What did I call the man now? Krala, was it? Kaala? Or Koralla, was it?

G. Krala.

J. He was a tall and more knowledgable man than I was. And he was the village merchant. And he liked me. He used to give me little things whenever he saw me, because he thought I was rather a—Ray, you weren't here?

Ray. No.

G. You weren't one of those people? They were all dark and you were fairish?

J. I was fair.

Ray. You went to the Middle East?

J. Yes. And I was a man!

Ray. Yeah?

J. I was a man—a tall skinny man. A sheep-herder of some kind.

G. Dirty and scruffy, too!

J. Scruffy, too! I had that dirty right *toe*nail! And I used never to bother to clean it.

Ray. *That* was quite something!

Leo. And she had complete conversations with people!

J. And I had complete conversations with people! Oh well, I can remember everything I said.

G. What was your face like again?

J. Hmm. Very long, like that—I can draw it better I think, I can draw it perfectly. (She started drawing, very quickly and skilfully.) I wore a simple white garment, to *there*, with a sort of blue and honey cord *there*! There was nothing elaborate about it. And a rough leather cord around it, and a white belt around it with a knife in it and *so* long. A knife with a curved handle. This was my one and only weapon and I used to make everything with it. It was my companion. I treated it like a companion. The staff was very simple and had a leather strap around my wrist. I went everywhere with the staff. I don't know of what it was made, but it felt strong and hard. It was very, very finely made, but it had flexibility in it. I don't know if it was metal—I didn't know about metals. But—I don't know what stories I used to tell the children. Whenever I went, the village liked to have me there to tell stories to the children. And when this man came to the village, the man they said was Jesus—Ray is starting to laugh now!

Ray. We were talking about this before it—

J. Before what? Tonight?

Ray. Yeah.

J. About Jesus?

Ray. Yeah. Anyway, carry on.

J. *Were* we?

G. Go on.

J. I didn't know him to be Jesus as *we* know him. He was just a man called Jesus who came to the village to talk to the people, and he had travelled many miles, and this man came and asked me to listen to him. They didn't know him, but he was a very good man who came to tell everybody stories about—

Ray. How old was he?

J. He was only twenty-three, and he had these coal-black luminous eyes. Fine features, but not particularly good-looking. More nondescript-looking. But he had these burning eyes looking at me and I knew; I thought, 'You'd better take those eyes *off* me because you're not going to *get* me', sort of thing. And the one desire I had was *not* going to listen to him. And I just felt selfish within myself, very determined I was, that I didn't want to stay and listen to him. I just had the feeling that if I somehow would become embroiled with him, he would stop me doing the things in my life I thought so pleasurable, like my goats, in my simple existence. I was a very happy soul and I didn't want—I *loved* my solitude, evidently. I *loved* it! This was overwhelming, right from the start. I was happy walking along the beach with a happiness of great simplicity, a great awareness of my earthy surroundings. I think I was even capable of communicating with the seagulls as they swerved past me. They sort of swooped at me as though they were companions rather than that I was a person. That was something I noticed. And the sheep, when they looked up at me, they looked as a *friend* and not as an animal does. The affinity I had with the animals! The donkey, and—and the children! The affinity was overwhelming within me! And I knew that *that* man wanted me to change my way of life to whatever he wanted of me. Whatever that was, I don't know. But I didn't want it! I was *very* determined about that. I think that was very evident. So I left the area where they were all gathered and went over to the wall and fell asleep.

We haven't had time to discuss this second trip of Joy's since that evening as, shortly afterwards, she had to fly suddenly to Melbourne for two weeks or so (she is there at the time of my writing this) to execute a rather sizeable and prestigious contract in interior decoration. I mention this to counter-balance, I hope, the suspicion I expressed at the beginning of this chapter; for if Joy had not been the responsible and very capable, as well as talented, person she is, she would not have been flown by an enormously successful businessman and world-traveller the two thousand miles or so from our small city of Perth to the much larger one of Melbourne.

But perhaps it was because of this very nature of Joy's that, for my next experiment, I chose a woman of roughly her own age but of very different (one might almost say the completely opposite) temperament. This time I chose someone who was very practical in her capability, not at all of an 'artistic' temperament and quite unsophisticated despite a certain amount of world travel; someone who has always been warm and congenial, and immeasurably fond of children and animals. As I expected from this next experimentee's very nature, there was nowhere near the graphic detail and colour there had been in both of Joy's runs; but if one can hold the experience to be the product of the imagination, then this experimentee's powers of imagination were certainly greater than Joy's.

Chapter Fifteen

Ruby B— had just turned forty-two years of age a few days before the experiment on the evening of the 1st of September, officially the first day of spring in Western Australia.

She has been widowed for over a year after eight years of a very happy marriage. Her husband, several years older than she, had been married before, and from this marriage had three daughters not so much younger than Ruby herself, and whom she had known, together with her husband's first wife, as well as her husband himself, for some time before he was widowed.

She has always been enormously fond of children and painstakingly patient with them, also with animals. I have known her to stop me killing a spider I had discovered inside the house; she then went to some considerable trouble to pick it up from the floor with a slim magazine and carry it out to the garden where she released it. When I asked her what she would have done if she hadn't had the magazine, or anything else with which to carry the spider, she said without hesitation that she would have picked it up in her hands, she was quite sure it wouldn't harm her.

When she was young, she had instructed girls in the Brownies and had previously been in the Girl Guides. She has always been popular with her own and the opposite sex, both treating her with deep respect yet thinking of her at the same time as a 'fun' person, someone with 'plenty of fun in her'. She had been devoted to her mother until the latter died, and was now equally attached to her elderly father. She was an only child, yet is quite unspoilt and has more the character of an *eldest* child of a large family than an only child. Probably no one would have relished it more than she if she had been.

Before her marriage she had had the one job with a smallish importing firm for several years and, when she was widowed suddenly and returned to her native Perth to look after her elderly father, she paid visits to her old employers as she did whenever she returned to Western Australia. They had always been pleased to see her and now this was proved by their offering her a position with them again. This she considered and accepted, despite the much greater travel involved since the firm's removal from the city.

I feel that I can truly testify as to her all-too-rare character for I have known her for almost twenty years and she has retyped the manuscripts of some of my books for me. One of them, *A Waltz Through the Hills*, is dedicated to her under her maiden name.

She was able to perform most of the preliminary exercises, the shrinking and expanding exercise reminding her, as it should have reminded me long before, of *Alice in Wonderland*; but she did have a little difficulty with visualization from the rooftop of the house in which she not only lives at present but had lived in from birth to womanhood before marriage. Yet she was able to ascend with ease. Her 'day' was cloudy and she soon passed above the clouds into brilliant sunlight, looking down on the marvellous cloudscape much as one does from a plane—except that she was quite adamant that there was no plane.

When I asked her to descend through the clouds, however, she said that she could see only ocean from horizon to horizon beneath her, dark in colour from the sullen overcast. She could see no land whatsoever. No islands, no rocks, no reefs. Nothing. Not even a ship. No kind of boat or craft whatsoever. 'Only the sea.' She was moving slowly across it, she said, at a very high altitude. But look where she would, she could see no sign of land whatsoever.

Remembering the admonition in the magazine *Open Mind* (to ensure that experimentees land on solid earth and not in water, lest they cannot swim and 'drown', or at least go through the motions of drowning, together with some of the hysteria expected to go with it), I asked if she could move in a different direction. She couldn't, so I asked her if there were still clouds above. There were; the sky was still completely overcast and dull. The air was cold around her but there was no wind. Could she ascend through the cloud again? She could, and did.

With her return above the clouds, she had again returned to brightness that was 'quite brilliant'. When asked if she could move across the cloud, she said that she could and was now doing so, looking for a gap somewhere to descend again, but as yet she couldn't find one. After a long silence, I asked her what she was doing and she said she was trying to find her way out of the cloud. She could see nothing but fog cloying around her, and she was very cold. Nevertheless she was quite content to continue trying to find her way down.

It took her a minute or so, but eventually she quite voluntarily said that she had 'come through them now'. What could she see? 'Still water.' No land? 'No land.' How high was she above the water? 'Oh, quite high.' I started to ask her what kind of sea it was now, but she interjected with 'It's as though I don't want to move.' Asked again about the sea, she said it was flat calm, she could feel no wind at all around her, there was no sign of wind. Yet she still felt cold.

Just as I was beginning to feel a little concern for the way this experience was developing, she told me that she could now see a little sunlight coming through the clouds. The sea was brightening. She could see some glimpses of sky through the clouds, and then the sun itself. And yes, she *could* move slowly over towards where there was a large break appearing in the sky. But below there was still only the ocean—water. There was no land or ship or anything else whatsoever.

From what viewpoint or embodiment did she think she was looking? She didn't know; it was 'just me'. The sea was still just flat calm with the sun now shining on part of it. But there was absolutely nothing else there. So far as I was concerned, I intended to heed my warning and not have her descend any further, let alone 'land' when there was nothing for her to land on. But then she volunteered, 'I'm still looking...'

Could she see any seabirds at all? 'No.' Could she come down just a little lower, to see if there might be some kind of life near, or perhaps just under, the surface? 'Yes.'

At this point, on the tape as I write this up now, there is the quite loud sound of a sports car decelerating outside, a sound which, when the tape was played back to her after the experiment was over, she said she could remember having heard at the time but that it hadn't at all distracted her. Yet it occurs to me now that it was more than loud enough to suggest some kind of speedboat. So I asked her what kind of noise had there been where she was over the ocean? 'Absolute silence.'

She was descending, very slowly and 'gracefully', till she was just above the surface, over which she was moving at a steady yet leisurely, almost a luxurious pace. But there was still nothing but sea. Above, the clouds had thinned further into 'little white fluffy clouds you see on a summer day, with the sun shining through brightly'. Apart from this, there was practically no change in her surroundings.

Was it still calm? 'Very calm.' And she was quite happy about being there? 'Very happy—there is something very calm and peaceful about the sea.' And it didn't frighten her at all? 'No.' Had she ever seen the sea look like this? 'Only from the window of a plane.'

And then I asked her was she aware that, while she was visualizing herself gliding over a calm sea, she was also remembering a sea she had seen from a plane in actuality? 'Yes.' And was she also aware of lying on my apartment floor telling about all this? 'Yes.'

Was there any point in her staying there longer? 'There's no point in it, except that it's beautifully calm and peaceful.' She could just go wherever she liked there? 'Yes.' She could move about as she wanted to? 'Yes.' Pause—and then I almost interrupted her, 'No one is there but me.'

After another long pause, I then ventured with, 'Say you are coming down gently—can you see your own feet?'

A very long pause and then, almost interrupted by me again, 'I think it's a bird.' Pause again, and then, 'You know how a bird comes down to land?' Yes, I said. 'Then I'm coming down a bit like that.'

Her voice was almost inaudible now, even awed. She appeared perfectly calm and contented. There was even a look of awed serenity on her face. Her eyelids were flickering rapidly and, beneath them, her eyes could quite clearly be seen moving from side to side and up and down. These movements were all very rapid indeed, so much so that I was surprised that they didn't distract her so much that her eyes would suddenly fly open and the experiment, *or* experience, would be over.

As she was coming down towards the surface, could she see

her feet at all? 'Not my *feet*.' Afterwards, she said she felt her legs were tucked up into her, well behind in her body, but she had thought this too absurd, or fantastic, to tell at the time. If she looked around her, to either side, could she see her shoulder or any part of her at all? 'Not of *me*.' Not of *you*? 'No.'

Could she see anything of herself at all?

'No, not really, but I imagine I must be a bird or something. Yes, a bird. I'm that close to the ocean, but I can go up high again'.

With relief, I repeated, 'Oh, you can go up high. Do you want to go up high?'

'No, not particularly. I'm quite happy where I am.'

'Do you look for anything? As you are over the sea?'

'No.'

'What do you think you would do if you wanted something to eat, or to drink?'

After a thoughtful pause, 'Well, as I'm a bird, I suppose I would get fish. But I don't know what I'd drink.' Another pause, and then, 'But it can't be very warm, because I'm cold.'

'You *are* cold?'

'Yes. Even though the sun's shining', she said, 'and I can see it sparkling on the water, I'm still cold.'

And indeed she was now shivering, although an electric heater was only three feet or so away from her, and in any case the night actually was not cold. I had Leo switch the radiator from medium to full heat, but she still shivered.

Could she feel any effect of wind at all?

'No.'

Could she hear anything? Was there any sound?

'Not over the water, no.'

'Do you hear any other sound?' She frowned at this, so I added, 'You can hear me talking, of course.'

'Mm!' Which she said quite readily, and then, 'I can hear the whirring the tape-recorder is making.'

'You don't hear any other sound?'

'The 'fridge just came on.' And this could be heard on the tape.

There was now, she said, no sun at all. Just clouds. The sea was still very calm and peaceful.

Could she see herself at all? No. Could she move freely still, and go back up to the clouds if she wanted to? Yes.

At this point another car could be heard starting up and departing, but Ruby immediately said, 'There's nothing I can see—there's nothing, no one else.'

'No one else?'

'No. I think I must be a bird.'

'And there's no other bird?'

'No. I'm all alone.'

'Do you look for anything, or are you just quite happy being where you are?'

'I don't know why I'm...I don't know why there's no one else there, or...or nothing else.'

'Does it seem something unusual? Or just a, you know, a normal thing?'

The sports car returned again, which made me note at the time that it must also have been the car departing recently, though its departure had been much less noisy than its arrivals. It had no apparent effect upon Ruby, whose eyes were still flickering and moving at the same rapid speed as previously.

'No, it doesn't seem unusual at all.'

A long pause again now, and so I asked her if she could go above the clouds again. 'Yes.' And she was already above them. So now I told her that she had her own choice: she could either come down to the sea again, or else she could come down through the top of the clouds to be over her own home. She decided to return to her home and said she was already descending, slowly. As, presumably, she did, she suddenly stopped shivering. She returned to the roof of her own home, observing aloud all the details of its features and garden as she landed. When I told her to, she opened her eyes and sat up—and the experience, of little less than an hour, was over.

It took her a few moments to recover; she said it was such a surprise to be back in my apartment and no longer over the sea. She would have been quite happy to have stayed there even though, she now confessed to me for the very first time, she had always been afraid not of birds in themselves but of the flapping of their wings. It terrified her. She couldn't bring herself to go near birds, not even common domestic fowls, if they could even move, let alone fly around. Yet she would feed fowls and wild birds, and had done so wherever she lived, provided she could keep well away from them.

We recorded all this and her voice had now resumed the lively nuances and qualities it normally had, instead of the flat low monotone I had come to accept as customary with these experiments.

'I'm not afraid of birds *stationary*. I'd feed birds anywhere,' she said. 'But the moment they take off and flap their wings, I'm frightened; even of a bird in a cage, flapping its wings.'

She then went on to say that once in Melbourne she had gone with a step-grandson and his father to a pet shop 'one Saturday to buy the dog's food, and in the shop in Croydon they had—oh, stacks and *stacks* of birds in cages, and I was looking at some rabbits underneath, and while I was looking someone came and did something to the birds and they all started flapping their wings and I just sort of—took off! My instincts are to cover my head like this'—and she covered her head with her arms—'from birds that flap their wings.'

I was astounded; over all the years I had known her, I had never heard her say anything about this phobia of hers—about the only one she has, I would say. It came as such a surprise in someone with her adoration of children and animals, indeed all creatures, for I knew her to have none of the customary fear of, say, snakes and spiders and such, nor even the customary feminine fear of mice. On the contrary, she herself then admitted that, while she keeps her large and old but redecorated house spotlessly clean, she would drop cheese to a mouse behind her refrigerator, saying, 'Well, *he* has to live *too*!'

I then asked her, when she had been a bird over the sea, had she then been afraid of other birds, or the flapping of their wings? Immediately and quite spontaneously she said, 'No.' She had forgotten it? 'I'd forgotten it. Or else I didn't know about it then.'

Did she think there was any connection with this and her experience just now?

'I don't know. I can't understand why the—well, *bird* was so uppermost, in my head. But that was what I just suddenly thought: could it be because I'm...not frightened of birds in themselves, but the moment they start flapping their wings or... a bird in flight, or a bird flapping its wings...and I get fright! I wouldn't go into the bird sanctuary in Queensland for that reason. I was all right while I could just stand outside, and look at them; but I wouldn't go in.'

Did she know what kind of a bird she had been? Something very large, *very* large, that glided, without flapping its wings, and was nearly always far away from any land, and *alone*, and in the cold part of the seas 'down south'. She had never seen a bird like the one she had been, although she had sailed from Australia to Japan and from there through South-East Asia—all tropical or at least warm seas. No name came to her mind, so Leo and I almost simultaneously prompted her with the albatross. Immediately she said, 'Yes, I think that's it.' So I then took the Encyclopaedia Britannica—and this, I think, just about explains, or confirms, just what *her* experience was:

> ALBATROSS, any of some dozen species of very large sea birds related to the petrels and constituting the order Diomedeidae in the order Procellariiformes. They have heavy bodies, exceptionally long narrow wings, a short tail in all except the sooty albatrosses (*Phoebetria*), short legs placed far back, large webbed feet without hind toe and a large stout hooked bill covered with horny plates, with a tube nostril on either side of the upper mandible. They inhabit colder oceans, often at great distances from land, nine species in lower parts of the southern hemisphere, one over cold waters off Peru and Ecuador and three in the north Pacific. The larger species (44–53 inches long) are known to sailors as gony, the smaller (28–37 inches long) as mollymawk or mallemuck.
>
> The largest species is the wandering albatross (*Diomedia exulans*), one of the two largest and most famous of flying birds, the other being the condor with smaller wingspread but heavier body. The great wandering albatross flies over circumpolar seas, 30° to 60°S, and breeds on subantarctic islands. It attains a length of 53 in., yellowish bill 7 in., wingspread 11·5 ft., and a weight of 20 lb. It is white, with faint wavy black bars on the mantle, and black tips to wings and tail. The sailors' superstition about killing an albatross was used in Coleridge's *Rime of the Ancient Mariner*. In regions of strong winds or gales albatrosses do not flap their wings but glide for hours low over rolling seas, settling on the water to feed on cuttlefish and squid, taking flight by fully extending their wings and running against the wind. With salt pork as bait, they are

caught on hook and line, cannot take flight from the deck, and become seasick with the roll of the ship. They rarely approach land, and breed on remote oceanic islands, rocky and inaccessible or low of coral sand.*

There is more about elaborate courtship performances, the laying and incubating by both parents of a single egg in a depression on the ground or in trampled grass, and of feeding its young (singular) on regurgitated food. Other information is of the other breeds or species in cold southern seas, and elsewhere, including the *Phoebetria* (perhaps Ruby should have been called Phoebe?)—more slender, graceful, and skilled in flight—in the cool south-eastern Atlantic ranging from South America to the Australian seas.

This revelation, of course, was quite shattering—even much more than when I myself had been 'coloured' and Joy had been a man instead of a woman. And yet, should I have been so surprised? After all, David K— had already affirmed to me, though it was not revealed at the time of his experience recounted in Chapter 10, that he felt sure he had been some kind of bird, probably some kind of eagle to have been able to dive and 'zoom around' as he had. I suppose it was the suddenness of Ruby's revelation, not so much the revelation itself, which took both Leo and me by surprise, for in a way we had been witnesses to its 'disclosure'. Yet Ruby herself seemed not at all surprised by the revelation, let alone dismayed. In fact, she accepted it in quite a matter-of-fact way. She even went so far as to say that, since the encylopaedia had revealed to her (and us) that an albatross did not flap its wings, but glided, it probably explained her fear (and also the albatross's?) of birds which do.

On questioning her about it all the following day, she was not only still quite undismayed by the revelation of her experience, but said she had no doubt that she had indeed been a large bird living over cold oceans far from land. What's more, she had been 'very very happy', with a feeling of peace that really had amounted to serenity, and she wouldn't at all mind 'being back there again'.

* Contributed by George Finlay Simmons, *Encyclopaedia Britannica* (Encyclopaedia Britannica, Chicago, 1961).

And yet there was to be still another surprise: she had come for the experiment not expecting anything to happen at all, even after having read part of the manuscript of this book beforehand; I had agreed to give her this because she had retyped manuscripts for me before and also because she would have the added 'ingredient' as an experimentee of being the first to have read something of what I had been doing prior to an experiment. Ah yes!—that immediately occurred to me, too. She had indeed read as far as Chapter 10, or David K— who had also gone 'flying', if in a very different way, and over land instead of only sea. But was that so very different after all? It didn't matter. When I consulted the typescript, I found that since only half of the chapter had so far been retyped, that is all she could have read. So she knew neither the outcome of David K—'s experience nor his subsequent explanations for it.

Yet this wasn't the end of surprises from her. Having read where several people had experienced cold when ascending through clouds and so forth, she had deliberately worn a long-sleeved spencer under a long-sleeved woollen jumper, together with woollen slacks, so that she, at least, 'would be prepared'. But she had still been cold, she said—as both Leo and I well knew.

Lastly, the following afternoon she came again to my apartment and we walked down to nearby Cottesloe Beach, she taking a brown paper bag of cake pieces and broken stale biscuits—to feed the seagulls. And she did it, even leaving the railed promenade to descend some steps to the lawn terrace immediately below so that she could break up some of the larger pieces of biscuits which, as we had seen, the seagulls had been unable either to swallow or break up for themselves. Yes, she was still rather frightened of them, she said. This was not at all surprising, as the seagulls were not only flapping around her but were shrilling, as is their custom, rather fiercely as well. But no, she wasn't as terrified as she had always been before.

No, she added, she didn't know yet whether or not she had been 'cured' of her fear, but she did feel she had at least acquired some sort of explanation for it. This had always eluded her before. In turn, it occurred to me that even if the experience was no such thing as a possible revelation of a past life nor even a particularly startling dream, it at least had the appearance of being quite a nice piece of psychiatric assistance. And so how, I wondered, would Freud have analysed, or even considered, this type of 'dream' when it was experienced in full consciousness?

Author's note in August 1974: Ruby avers her fear of birds flapping their wings to be nowhere near so great as it had been prior to her Christos experience. She still has a little discomfort from them, but no fear.

Chapter Sixteen

After Ruby, I really felt—and still do feel—that I had enough experiments to satisfy any reader, whether his interest be genuine or merely entertainment; but only two days later on Friday, September 3rd, and the thirty-second anniversary of the Second World War, no less than three more experimentees came within my 'clutches' and, tired though I was, having just come out of hospital, I 'took' them just the same; the three within nine hours of each other, or between three in the afternoon and midnight.

Colin N— at thirty-seven is an unmarried manager of a cinema, after a good many positions in a varied career of which, he says, the only stable factor is being (like myself, incidentally) a Sagittarian. He is of average height and build, dark-haired but fair-complexioned, wears glasses because of severe astigmatism in one eye while the other is near-perfect. He owns his apartment which is tastefully furnished and is the possessor of several original paintings from such renowned local artists as McDiven and Juniper. He shares this apartment with a younger geologist friend from another state who is mostly away 'in the field' in outback Western Australia with a metals exploration company. Colin is interested in astral travelling which he has attempted several times but says that he has succeeded only as far as being able to look down on his own body where it was lying in a room; so far he has been unable to get himself even outside that room, which he has found very frustrating. This last information, however, he did not volunteer until the experiment was over.

It was carried out in my apartment one dullish afternoon when he called in unexpectedly; he barely had the time for the experiment and I rather hurried the preliminaries with little explanation beforehand, which is probably why I at least found it somewhat disappointing. I am recounting it here because he himself was very impressed with it, for it had, he said, enabled him to go 'so much further' beyond himself than any of his attempts at astral travelling. Later, he was to witness American Jim McA—'s 'run' and then immediately remarked that Leo and I must have found his own experience dull indeed by comparison; however, he averred, it was still very vivid and meaningful to him. It was tape-recorded but, because of the way this book is mounting up, I am considerably paraphrasing this and the next two experiences.

He accomplished most of the preliminaries with ease but had difficulty with ascending. Instead of ascending above Perth somewhere, he found himself immediately above Sydney, seeing the bridge and opera house. When he went higher, he was engulfed by cloud and then, to his surprise (for he very perceptibly jumped) he bumped against something 'concrete' in the cloud with his left shoulder, something like a concrete pillar, he didn't know what. It took him some time to avoid it and to be able to descend through the cloud, but when he did it was to his obvious delight, if not relief. When he descended again, it was a 'brilliant day with a bright blue sky' and he was in a rural district somewhere with very green fields. Everything around him was very clear, almost unbelievably so. I then asked him if he was seeing with or without his glasses, and immediately he was confused. 'I don't know,' he said. 'I don't think it matters—now. I can see quite well without them.'

Asked to look down at his feet when he had landed (after seventeen minutes since commencement), he said he was wearing suede or 'desert-boot' type shoes (when in actuality he was in his socks, having removed ordinary leather shoes). The grass around him, of which he could see every blade and seed, was about four inches high. He thought it was a wheat crop. Above his boots, he could not see anything he was wearing, but he must have been wearing *something* as he couldn't see his bare legs either. He was more interested in his surroundings; he was in a very large field or paddock, bounded by a fence made of rough-hewn wooden posts strung with wires, and filled with wheat. Beyond were low and undulating hills with few trees. The only habitation was an old farmhouse, not so far away, built of stone with a roof of rusty iron which might have been painted red at some stage. He was approaching from the back of the building which had no other buildings around it. He didn't think he had ever seen it before in actuality, but he *had* seen buildings *like* it, near Geraldton almost four hundred miles north of Perth.

He was now walking round to the front of the farmhouse. Here it had a large veranda and there was a road passing quite near by. A truck was passing, one belonging to 'Master's Milk' (a local dairy). The house, he could now see, was indeed quite deserted and very overgrown. There was no one else anywhere around. He had never lived or even stayed there and he didn't particularly want to go inside. What would be the point? So I had him ascend again, changing from day to night and back to day again, then trying to land once more. He had been eight minutes at the deserted farmhouse. He spent another two minutes or so above Perth, by both day and night, before descending again.

I asked him who had changed day to night and back to day again. As had become customary, he answered, 'I did, when you suggested it.' He was perfectly aware of his actual surroundings and was almost scornful when I asked him if he had any suspicion of hypnotism or any other psychological control being exerted on him. He was, he said, quite able to do just whatever I asked him to do—ascend, descend, see by night or day, or even terminate the experiment.

It was now a brilliant day and he was over the ocean. There was no land anywhere, he thought, and naturally I immediately surmised that we were about to have another experience like Ruby's. However, this one was to be very different after all. Presently he could see a lighthouse on a lone and very small rock, and almost automatically he was descending towards it. Indeed, he actually landed before I asked him to do so. He could feel the rock underneath his feet which this time were bare, the skin wrinkled as though they had been in water for some time. He was white-skinned but tanned, when normally he tans very little. At first he thought he was wearing 'shorts', but then he wasn't sure; what he was wearing was just a brief but indeterminate undergarment. He was walking around on the rocks which were dry and firm and smooth, brownish. There were no plants or shells or even seaweeds of any kind.

The sea was intensely blue, calm, sunlit. There were birds now —seagulls.

When asked how big the rock in the ocean was, he said it was hard to tell from his present viewpoint, and so without any suggestion from me he ascended above it to look down. It was about the size of a house, he said—very small, just big enough to hold the lighthouse. There was no land, no other rocks, not even reefs anywhere around—just this one rock and the lighthouse. The lighthouse was neither modern nor very old. He neither worked nor lived there. He had just 'arrived'. He could go *to* the lighthouse, but not inside it. He couldn't see a door, nor find one when he walked round it. It was made of rusty red steel, riveted, not welded, and had probably been daubed with red lead long ago. It had a cat-walk but he couldn't see if the lighthouse still worked as such or not; he thought not, and certainly not during the day, which it then was. He was quite sure, now, that he had never seen it before, in either actuality or dream. He was also sure that there was nobody in it. There was still no sign of ship or boat all round. He was alone. He was walking round the concrete base of the lighthouse, again looking for a door, but there wasn't one. Clouds were now closing in around him and he was suddenly aware of wearing a green shirt, which he did not actually possess, and shorts of a greyish colour which were much like what he would choose in reality, but he could not say that he did have this particular pair, or had ever had them.

While he was telling me this, he said he had started to 'float' and thought he was knocking into the concrete pillar he had encountered before in the clouds. No, it was definitely not the lighthouse; that was made of steel, whereas this, whatever it was (for he couldn't see it), was definitely made of concrete. It bore no relation to the lighthouse. He was now far up in the clouds but could still remember the lighthouse very vividly; at the same time he was perfectly aware of lying in my apartment and was quite conscious of the sounds and occasional movements around him. The telephone had rung in another room and Leo had gone to answer it, but this hadn't distracted him; it had been 'no concern of his'. He was now almost completely enveloped in cloud, very high up, but with just the one small opening through which, very far below, he could still just see the lighthouse which was now quite diminutive. He didn't want to return to it and he couldn't determine whatever it was that he kept bumping into, 'not when it was just up in the clouds—what would be the point?' Besides, he said, the sky had cleared and he was descending once more on a brilliantly sunny day.

This time there was land beneath him all round. It was desert. Again he landed quickly on the desert sand. He couldn't actually 'feel' it, but he was 'there'. He was in a small valley of yellow sand with a blazing blue sky above. No cloud. There was absolutely nothing else. He felt warm, but he couldn't see anything of himself; he didn't seem to have any 'form'. He thought he was floating, while lying down, prostrate. It was as though he was sleeping, yet he knew he wasn't asleep. The sandy valley he was in was very small, only about the size of a room. The sand was constantly drifting. He didn't know which part of the world it might be, but he was able to rise up out of the 'valley', or sand-pit, to float just above the surface and could see for miles around. It was *all* just desert, with yellow sandhills rolling for miles around, without sign of any tree, let alone habitation. Again, as twice before, he was completely alone—but now he had no form either. He rose high again, and at once found himself in some kind of aeroplane, but a very small one, with no one in it but himself for he was in the cockpit. The plane was spinning over 'harsh looking' ground, but after a while both this ground and the plane were gone. He was drifting down. He drifted formlessly down into his own body in the room in my apartment and was back.

I felt that this rather hurried experience had failed, but he disagreed. It had all been very vivid, he said, as in the most vivid of his dreams. The scenes at the lighthouse and in the desert had been 'timeless'—he had no idea whatsoever how long ago it might have been. But he himself was excited at having succeeded in going further beyond himself than he had in his previous attempts at astral travelling, which he only now told me about. One point was very clear to him: each of the three times he had been alone, without even seeing any other people—and that's how he felt his 'present' life mostly was.

Mrs Julie W— was married just four months before the experiment, a few days after her nineteenth birthday, and now lives with her husband, a schoolteacher not yet twenty-two at the time of writing, in a small country town about three hundred miles north of Perth where he is appointed to a state secondary or high school. Julie helps her husband with a good deal of his work, having herself won both a Commonwealth (of Australia) scholarship and an American field scholarship, though marriage prevented her from taking advantage of the latter award. After leaving school, she worked as a clerk for a year. She is, by any standards, very nearly beautiful. She is also charming, vivacious and intelligent, and devoted both to her young husband and, it seems, to his work too. I have known her husband, Geoff, for four years since he was at school himself. His parents have been the kindest and most helpful neighbours I have known anywhere over a good many years. The young couple, both of whom I consider good and close friends, were here for a few days while he took examinations all day over the weekend. On the Friday night, after dinner, they called on me for coffee and 'just ten minutes' chat.

Whenever they return to Perth they invariably ask about my work; and so when they were told about the experiments I was doing, Julie, immediately and eagerly, volunteered. And so they stayed until midnight.

She was especially quick with the preliminaries, so much so that I thought she was going to 'be off' long before she should. While describing the surroundings from the rooftop of their new country home, she said that she found there was an image of another building, and of a hill, under the buildings that were there in reality. The hill, particularly, persisted when it wasn't there in reality. She had never seen it before, nor the older building behind the school building, but she believed this other building had once existed before their arrival there. So far as she knew, the hill had never been there. This was the only oddity in otherwise fast and facile preliminaries until, when she had ascended to the clouds and was asked what was above them, she immediately said 'a roof'. She was no longer up in the clouds but was already down on earth without being asked to descend. I shall now paraphrase considerably, but using her own words as from Leo's transcript of the tape.

She was looking up at a roof. 'The window is *there*! A round window! And it's got—panes? No, no—bars. Tall. I think I'm on a farm. I am lying on the bed. I can see my head, but it's *not* my head as it is now. I'm younger. I'll be twelve. Blonde hair (hers is very dark brown, straight and longish), short, a bit curly. Can't see my eyes. I have big hands—big for my age. There is nothing on them (in fact she was wearing two rings, one on each hand, and a wristwatch). I am wearing a nightgown. Very long, white, and it's got big frills around it at the bottom. And it comes right down to the floor. And it's got long sleeves, with frills. I've got short hair. Very short. Half-way between straight and curly. Blue eyes. I'm not asleep. I'm lying down there on my bed and I'm looking up at the ceiling. It is like this (and she made a peak with her hands)—gabled. No supports. No rafters. The walls seem to be only four feet high at the sides. It must be a bedroom under a roof. An upstairs bedroom. There's a wooden floor. The stairway is over there. (She pointed *down* from my floor to the left.) Not very big, the room. It's *not* very big. About a square (one hundred square feet in Australia, and approximately ten square metres). I have a single bed, no foot or head, nothing. A mattress, straw. A rug over it. I'm lying on the top of it, not *in* it. There is a stool. And a rough window—there (she pointed ahead of her)—which has got bars on it. Both horizontal and vertical, like panes. And the stool—a small stool, wooden, no back, four legs. Further there is nothing. Oh, the top is leather. It's very old. *Very* old! The *building* is very old. Yes, I'm on a farm. I have one parent. The hill! The *hill* I saw—is out the window! To the right. It's the one I saw at the school in the sunset, before. And now when I look out of this little window, I can see the hill.

My parent is my father. I can see him, below. He's wearing a shirt, long pants and boots. He's about thirty, blond, short curly hair, like mine. Blue eyes. He doesn't have a beard or anything—he's clean-shaven. But at the moment he's got—whiskers? Stubble! (She didn't know his name, nor her own.) I can see him downstairs. Inside. Standing in the kitchen, in the doorway. He has just come inside, from working. (At that stage there was just herself and her father, no one else; but then she corrected herself.) Yes, there is a woman, but she is not my mother. An old woman? No, no. She's got on a blue dress, and she has got her hair tied in something, like a scarf, like...like women wear when their hair's up in curlers, something like that. She's got a long dress on, blue, down to her ankles. Right down. She is standing in the kitchen. She is doing something there, making, making—she is near an oven. She is making something to eat, I think it must be soup. Or boiling meat, or something like that. She is big—not big, but big shoulders. She is not my mother, though. And she isn't married to my father. They are exactly the same age. (I then asked her where she herself was as she had assumed a puzzled and then a worried frown, almost anxiety.) I'm down in the kitchen. I'm dressed in boys' clothes. Pants and shirt, no shoes. I think—I think my father and I have got—for a belt—a rope. Not string. Long trousers, and no shoes. The floor is wood. It's cold. It's lunchtime now. (She didn't go to school.) I work on the farm. (Afterwards she added, 'Like a boy. Dressed as a boy. That's why I like to lie in my nightgown in the morning. I'm a *girl* then!') Sometimes by myself, sometimes with my father. Around the farm, with chickens. Just chickens. It's a small farm. I see a dog. It is black and white. It is a small dog, shabby. (I asked if it had a name.) No. (Then, suddenly, and just as suddenly breaking the quiet and customary monotone of her voice, she almost exploded with 'Bill!'; she admitted afterwards that she had made this up just to please *me*, but she was unable to continue with the pretence.) It is not my dog; it's my father's dog. I don't like the dog. I don't like it. (Afterwards, she and her husband hastened to tell me of her fear of all dogs, so perhaps it was a pity I did not have her pursue this line instead of asking her if the time was the present.) No. It's a hundred years ago. About that. In America. I'm American. It's a poultry farm in the middle of America. (Afterwards, she said it was in Kansas; if I myself had a map she could show me.) And it is very dry. Just grass. No trees. No trees on the hill. Just grass. Yellow grass. There is a poultry yard, here. With hens. All different colours. Mainly white. The house is behind me. The hill is still there, what you can see from the kitchen window. It's a part of the yard. Poultry farm here, hill there! I don't know what is in front of me. The dog is standing by my side. And the hill is just there—so that I can see it from my bedroom window. Fifty yards away. (She could easily get to the top of it. What did she see from there?) Just grass. No other buildings or farms. Just grass. Behind, there is another farm. A poultry farm. I don't know the people.

'Are you happy in the farm?'

'No.'

'Are you happy with your father?'

'Yes.'

'But you don't like being on the farm?'

'No.'

Afterwards she said that she felt she ought to have told me something when she had first seen her father, then the woman, downstairs in the kitchen, but she had been apprehensive about it. There had been a terrible tension in the household, she said, especially between her father and the woman, the housekeeper. Not between her and her father. But also between her and the woman. Her father slept with the woman, but he didn't want to marry her. Now he didn't want her there at all. He wanted her to go but she wouldn't leave. She made it unbearable for everyone, especially 'myself, as my father's daughter'.

'Do you want to do something else? Do you want to go away?'

'No.' (Tentatively, undecided.)

'You want to *stay* there?'

'No, but I'm too young to go anyway, about twelve. My moth—'

I fear then I interjected with, 'Is there any kind of township nearby?'

'No. We are here all alone. We seem to be all alone.'

'What did you want to say about your mother?'

'She's dead.'

'Do you know how?'

'In childbirth, I think. The woman, I think, is just a housekeeper, and she doesn't get on with my father...'

She didn't say anything for a long time, then her eyes opened and she was back. Although she immediately stood up from lying on the floor, she said she was exhausted and slumped into a chair. Nevertheless, she was most eager to talk.

'How long do you think you have been?' I asked her.

'Five minutes.'

'No, half an hour.'

She was incredulous. 'Half an hour altogether?'

'No, since you "landed".'

I then asked her if it had been as clear as, say, a dream.

'A lot clearer. Nearly no colours.'

'*No* colours?'

'Except for the blue dress, the yellow grass, that's all. And my nightdress was—white. And those were the only colours. Everything else was just—black and white...'

But later she recalled many more colours and recounted more details that she had not wanted to tell about at the time. She had even resented my intrusions as she wanted to 'see everything and not talk about it in case she missed seeing something'. We talked for a little while longer, her incredulous young husband plying her with numerous questions. Then, despite the lateness of the hour, he said he wanted a run too, to see, not what his young wife had seen, but *how* she had seen it.

Geoff W— has already been introduced as Julie's husband.

The preliminaries took him only fifteen minutes instead of the usual twenty or more, but he then spent an hour floundering through what was easily the most confusing variety of settings experienced so far. He thought he had landed on something half-way between a desert and New York City, if you can imagine that, with one of the buildings leaning over him almost horizontally—a building of brick and steel and glass in which there were no people and he himself could not enter. Then he realized that he was standing opposite the building and was almost the same length, several hundred feet long or so. When he looked down, he could clearly see his bare feet, huge, yet in proportion with the rest of his enormously elongated body. His feet seemed suspended above what looked like swampy green grass. Then, to the left, there suddenly appeared a vertical array of brownish terraced houses. On his right was a vertical or perhaps hanging park. The latter, incredible as it sounded, was vivid in both forms and colours, distinctly a park, with trees and ponds, 'ducks and things' and just about everything a park could have. There were people in and around both the terraced houses and the park, but none in the building. It was as though he was seeing a four-sided well, a square well, with himself as one side of it. When asked to concentrate again on his feet and the grass beneath them, his bare feet slowly disappeared and the bottom of the well immediately became its top—as though the well, like a sock, had been pulled inside out. Yet the grass was still growing above him, so that he looked through its white and yellowish roots to the green blades and then *through* the grass to the bright blue sky beyond.

The building, park, terraced houses and himself had now all become the sides of the well, and yet he was also down at the bottom of it looking up. He could no longer see anyone else at all. And now as he looked up, as well as the 'inverted' grass at the top of the well he could also see railway sleepers; and through all this the sky, or at least glimpses of it. He was cold and a little wet down in this well, from water dripping down its sides. He was especially wet on his bare legs. He didn't know if he had any clothes on at all. The sun, coming down through the sleepers, was beginning to annoy him, it had become so bright. Indeed its light was almost white, nearly blinding him. He couldn't get himself up out of the well, and yet in actuality he had never been down one in his life before. Now he could see he was wearing black shorts (I am beginning to think that the Australian very brief black football shorts are an Australian's symbol of masculinity!). He wore nothing else. His legs were darkish from the water and the dimness in the well, but he himself wasn't dark. He was European, white. His shorts were very old and 'all torn' and now he had an old shirt on too, possibly one he might once have had in reality. He was now his normal height, or even smaller, and about ten years of age.

The base of the well had broadened out into a cavern, the roof descending upon him, yet still with the grass and the railway sleepers above him in one direction. Asked if he could now get out of wherever he was, he said he didn't know, because he didn't know where the exit was, but he did have to find it. He was already appearing tired and frustrated, confused. The sides of the cavern, once a well, were of rough and dark rock dripping with water. There was a little sand here and there, and a small stream he would have to walk through to go the way he wanted to go. The water was up to his ankles and disappeared into the darkness. Then, as he walked, he encountered a dog's skeleton lying on the sand with an old hessian bag near it.

He felt he was now not only in the cavern but also under a bridge, a railway bridge, which explained the railway sleepers from before as these were still there. The grass, however, had entirely disappeared. The bridge was very tall so that it was a long way up to the railway line. When he looked down, he was again confronted by the bony remains of the dog. When he looked up, he was again blinded by sun. I checked the room's lights but there were only the two normal table-lamps switched on, no overhead lights, and of course it was night-time. Yet he was obviously having trouble with glare, to the extent of squinting up his closed eyes and shading them with his left hand. He was making his way along the stream, feeling the cold of the water and the sharpness of the coarse sand on his bare feet (in actuality he moved his feet a lot now, while his hands wavered aimlessly, almost hopelessly, around). When asked if he could see his own face now, he replied, 'Snub nose, freckles.' He was about ten. He had ginger hair, straight, slanting forwards. (This is nowhere near his actual appearance which is blond, slim, long-nosed.) It took him some time while floundering around in the well/cave/hollow-under-a-bridge, but he eventually realized his name was Peter.

He had now found his way out of the cavern and on to rocky ground, still under the bridge, which appeared to be built across a 'sink-hole', as he called it, but which after some time resolved itself into, or else was recognized by him as, an open-cut mine of some kind; probably, from his description, it was a coal-mine. He was no longer barefooted; he was wearing boots, black, like army boots. He wasn't sure yet about the rest of his clothes as he was now busy, and relieved, looking around. The open-cut mine rose up darkish and on various levels on all four sides, square, like the well had been; but now this was a much broadened-out version of what the well *might* have been. The railway bridge still straddled it. Beyond it he 'knew' there was some kind of a town, or even a city, which he thought was inhabited by 'kind of Asians—you know, Mongols maybe, but not just Chinese, browner than Chinese, and taller'.

He thought, as the ten-year-old Peter, that he was still in Western Australia, somewhere near a place called Bushmead where he had once played as a boy and seen a somewhat similar yet different railway bridge. But at the same time he thought he was now a man, a grown man, thirty or forty, tall, dark, well-built, French. Or maybe French-Canadian. His name started with a 'zshee' (as distinct from a 'gee' or a 'jay') but he couldn't pronounce this new name of his. It wasn't Jean, or Jean-something. Jacques? Yes, that was it—it was Jacques. Definitely—Jacques.

He was in the cold of Canada when he was on this other side of the mine, for when he walked up from the creek at the bottom of the mine he changed from the boy Peter to the man he was now, in boots and lumberjack-style jacket and lumberjack shirt, and a kind of hunting or perhaps 'Sherlock Holmes' style of cap. He was a hunter. He lived entirely by hunting. He was walking up to the top of the mine, towards where he knew the Asian-type city would be. And when he looked down to where he had been, he could still see the boy Peter whom he had previously been. Then, conversely, his 'mind', or his 'self', could 'leap' back into himself as the boy Peter and look back up at his other self, the man Jacques, as the latter, walking along the top of the mine, was sharply silhouetted against the still-blinding glare! The man was going towards the city, so he chose to be 'in' the man. But when he was asked to choose either the man or the boy to stay in all the time, he suddenly found himself back in the boy, running off barefooted to his bicycle (which he hadn't had before) in Bushmead, yet not in Bushmead, to go home to a home he knew to be there somewhere, but was not a home in which he had ever lived in actuality. And, after an hour of indecision that both confused and irritated him, he too was back.

He remained somewhat confused by it all, though his wife could see some of his 'real self and past' in the boy Peter, which he immediately contradicted. He could see more now of the city he *hadn't* visited while he had been 'away'; but now he realized that it had been more like a vertical and painted back-drop as on a stage, yet with real people moving about in it. It had been warm there, though it had been cold on the other side of the 'sink-hole' or mine where Canada had been. And somewhere there had been an English-style cottage. The man was at the top of the mine, the boy at its bottom after having been both in the cavern and at the bottom of the well. The one 'realistic' thing in these somewhat surrealistic surroundings, he said, had been the incredible discovery that he could, as himself, leap from man to boy and back again, innumerable times, just whenever he wanted to, sometimes even being caught, or stopping, between the two, and being able to regard both. Perhaps, it occurred to both him and me, that was precisely what he was still doing now in reality or in his 'present life', call it what you will; he was reluctant to make up his mind which, of course, simply had to be 'made up'. Furthermore, he felt that both the boy Peter and the man Jacques had not only lived in different and distant parts of the world, but also at different and perhaps just as distant times. It had given him a lot to think about and he and Julie would both like to try the experiment again. But as it was midnight they were sent home instead.

Chapter Seventeen

Jim McA—, twenty-five, single, was born of Scottish stock in Toledo, Ohio, in the United States. We met a few months previously while he was a transient tourist in Perth doing a round-the-world walking and working tour; in other words hitch-hiking whenever he could to preserve his limited funds, and working wherever he could to refurbish them. He had been away from home for about fifteen months and expected to be about two years altogether before returning to employment in Chicago. Prior to this journey, he had also travelled a fair amount within the United States with his family and relatives, from childhood on. He is the youngest of three sons, in a family he described as 'very close', the other two brothers being married.

His occupation is store designer which he was able to apply immediately upon arrival here to one of the city's largest stores. He graduated from the University of Toledo with a B.A. in marketing. He then, at twenty, spent a year in Chicago at an art school before starting his career there as a store designer. Both in the States and while travelling he smoked marijuana, and it was for his knowledge of the various kinds from the world that I wanted him for an experimentee. The experiment was carried out one mild spring evening in my apartment with two other witnesses who had already been run (Ruby and Colin).

He took the average time of twenty minutes over the preliminaries, which gave him no difficulty, or so we thought until it was time to bring him down to 'land'. I was then disappointed to find he had come down over the Arc de Triomphe in Paris which he could describe in impressive detail, as he had with his visualization exercises from the flat he has rented here, in what is a 'foreign country' to him. I was even more disappointed to find that he didn't *want* to land because the traffic around the arch would probably 'kill him'. But then we discovered that, unlike every other experimentee, he had not automatically 'deflated' from his expansion exercise while studying his front door. He was still enormous, he said—like a giant, so that his toe alone would crush the arch. Realizing what had happened, I had him ascend again and then re-descend. He came, 'like Jack and the beanstalk', down a gigantic vine as, now that he was small again and not a giant as before, he was afraid of falling.

For a while I thought he had made another false start when he said he was coming down over a village in Australia, the association being even more recent than his visit to Paris just over a year ago. Also, there are no 'villages' as such in Australia, which I suppose should have shown me that the fault had been in my own hearing—for it was soon obvious that he had meant Austria and not Australia. After a while, he was even able to pinpoint the village to Salzburg, but a very strange Salzburg it was.

The setting, with the mountains to the south, was much the same as it is now; but when he landed on the cobbled courtyard or square, seeing the cobbles and their patterns with a clarity that obviously surprised him, he said that the 'village' of Salzburg was very small indeed. It consisted of just a few buildings, one the remains of a castle and another a church in ruins but with twin towers with gold and turquoise spires. These towers perplexed him as he thought churches should have only the one. We told him afterwards that many Austrian and Bavarian churches did have two and then mostly 'twin', in the sense of identical, towers or spires.

There was a fountain behind him, but it wasn't working as it was still boarded up from having been protected from the winter. There were other buildings and shops on one side of the church, but opposite it there was nothing but a great devastation as though, in his own words, 'it had been bulldozed to build an airport'.

Was he still in modern times after all? But no, evidently not; for when I asked him if it were an airport being built there, his immediate reply was a scornful laugh, 'Oh, no! That would be ridiculous!'

After a while, because he could see no people anywhere, except one old man trundling an empty cart out of the village, he began to think that some dreadful catastrophe, like an earthquake or something of that nature, had indeed befallen the village with the consequence that its entire population had fled.

We then realized which period of time he was 'in' by his description of his clothes—tall, square-toed, suede boots with wide floppy tops, 'tights' of some indeterminate material, a thigh-length jacket. This dress, together with his long and dark straight hair (his actual hair is fair and straight, and of medium length) and his black pointed beard, seemed to indicate a period around the thirteenth century.

He felt he was dressed as some kind of 'comic', but he didn't feel comic at the moment; instead, his head felt 'very heavy'. He was much older, at least 'thirty-nine or more', for his long hands had the wrinkled skin of a much older person than he was now, so that in reality—or, rather, in the reality of his experience—he was probably nearer his fifties or even sixties than thirty-nine. He did not wear glasses in the experience, as he did in reality.

He now started to leave the village and he was impatient with me for asking for more descriptions of a church that was empty and abandoned. However, on his way out of the village through a narrow and still cobbled street, he did see another person other than the old man who had now trundled his empty cart out of sight. This was a buxom woman of thirty or more, wearing a wide, white, bonnet-type hat with starched sides coming round her face, and 'a low square-necked white blouse-affair with a black harness-looking square-necked dress'. As he approached her, she waved to him enticingly from a second-storey casement window above a bakery or *patisserie*. But whether she was enticing him to buy these wares or her own he was not certain. In any case, he had already passed her and was leaving the village.

The cobbled street had given way to a mere dirt track in which he could clearly see the ruts from carts and the trampling from horses. These ruts were sometimes filled with water and the track itself was very muddy. All round him the landscape was wet, as though it had rained shortly before. The air was cool, crisp. From the pale-green shoots of trees and bushes here and there, he was quite sure that it was early spring. Surrounding fields were mostly of dark, wet, rich-looking earth without, as yet, any crops appearing in them, though later on this gave way to barren, arid ground where nothing could be grown. Ahead were mountains, with snow-capped peaks that reminded him of the one depicted by Paramount Pictures.

From being slightly overcast, the sun was now coming out. He was still walking, sometimes loping, along, though his head was still heavy. He had, too, a pain at the back of his neck; and in actuality he stretched and rubbed it, then passed his hand over his forehead. Yet he kept on walking along the rough mud track away from the village.

He felt compelled to keep on walking, though as yet he had no idea of where he was going. Sometimes he felt inclined to leap and jump, despite his age. He couldn't explain this inclination to 'act like Ray Bolger in Judy Garland's *The Wizard of Oz*' just as he couldn't explain his compulsion to keep on walking, nor why he should have his headache and the pain in his neck.

Then the road turned and he arrived at water. At first he was confused, thinking it was the sea because there were fishing-boats anchored near a small village. But then he realized that the water was a pond or a lake. The same mountains were still beyond. The village had a small inn in front of which he could see some people tethering horses to a rail, then going inside. It was an old, long building—very old. He felt that he wanted to go in too, as he was thirsty.

I deliberately did not press him at this point but let him remain silent for some little while, to make his own choice. When I did ask him what he was doing, he said he had passed the inn and the village, even though he was still terribly thirsty, because for some reason or other, he didn't know what, he hadn't wanted to go in with the other people and felt compelled to walk on to wherever he was going.

The way was still rough and muddy as he circled the pond with rushes and water-lilies. There was a strange boat left inexplicably abandoned in it.

His head was still heavy. It seemed to be getting heavier and heavier. He still had the pain in his neck. He felt depressed within himself, but not at all by the experience itself; the depression was merely how he had felt at that time. And he still didn't know where it was he was going; he was just following this road.

It was spring, but there was little apart from clover in the fields now, and everything was still wet from the recent rain. There was snow up on the mountains. He was still dressed as before, his green suede boots now quite wet and muddy round the soles.

The land was now hilly and rising, becoming barren again with little growth. But ahead, far away, there was a small clump of trees—'very far away'—and this was where, he now knew, he had to go.

He was now 'frolicking' along, although he felt he was in a kind of stupor, dazed, perhaps from some shock, he didn't know what. There was also pressure on his head, but at that time, or perhaps now as well, he couldn't tell. He kept jumping up and down and couldn't stop himself despite the pain in his head, just as he couldn't stop himself from continuing along the road. Perhaps he was jumping up and down to 'shake out' the pain from his head.

He was trying to get to the clump of trees as fast as he could, but they were still some way off though discernibly nearer. It seemed a small clump; but even the size of the clump appeared to increase as he approached, still jumping along with his headache.

We all went through an almost step-for-step description of this jolting and jumping journey of his, but eventually the clump of trees did come nearer, and grew much larger, as he headed towards it and entered what became a sizeable forest.

The trees were tall and thin, pines or firs possibly, 'a bit like redwood trees but with trunks without boles and which seem to go straight up, all the same width and *very* close together'. So close together were they, the sunlight was almost completely obliterated. It was now difficult for him to see. It was also, suddenly, very much colder there in the dark of the forest.

At one point, he thought he heard threatening 'grumbling' noises, but could see neither person nor creature. Yet he felt someone was 'gawking' at him. But he was pushing his way through the trees and the dense undergrowth, still with his headache and neck pain.

He had to get out of this forest, he said several times. And his body was now writhing somewhat on my apartment floor when, for some time before, it had been merely his socked feet moving as though he was indeed jumping and leaping about. His face was now obviously screwed up with anxiety—or perhaps desperation, or even terror—and I wondered if I should bring him out of this experience which had already lasted an hour. But when I suggested this he barely listened, saying he wanted to go on to see where it was that he was going to and what it was that, he now knew, he was going to do when he arrived 'there'. So I let him go on.

The sunlight was almost completely obliterated now as, apart from the denseness of the forest, there was a thick fog seeping down through the trees. He could barely find his way. The noises had faded away behind him, without being identified, as he pressed on. Then abruptly he stopped. And on my apartment floor he was as abruptly still.

He had arrived at a ledge, he said. He couldn't see down, but he knew he was at the edge of a cliff, or chasm. And this was what he had come there for—this ledge. He wanted to jump.

Again I started to restrain him, fearing the results that the article in the magazine *Open Mind* had warned me about and not wanting a young American corpse on my carpet. But somehow I felt that, as with a dream, there was little chance of any danger coming to an experimentee even if he or she did apparently die during the experience, for hadn't Joy turned out to have been already 'dead' in a much earlier experiment? Despite Jim's slim build, he looked and seemed fairly healthy to me and not at all a candidate for a heart attack, let alone heart failure. So again I let him go on.

'What's down below?' I asked him.

'I can't *see*! But I *want* to jump off! Yeah, I'm *going* to jump off! What is it with these trees! The trees just stop when they come to this ledge! But I want to *jump*! I feel like I'm floating. It's too late, I can't get back! I'm falling head over heels! I'm not falling fast, I'm falling very lightly. Very—' he paused, then breathed slowly and deeply several times—'just like a slow-motion film of someone falling. I'm still going down. It's still cloudy. Like a big haze of clouds. (Pause) Hope it's not—strange!'

'Are you still going?'

'I'm still falling.'

'Just slowly?'

Almost marvelling, 'Just slowly! I like it. I like it because it's like—weightlessness. Very, very light. *Oh*, I've got a headache! (Pause, and he breathed out heavily.) Now as I'm going I think I'm coming down. (Pause) I'm not, I'm still floating.'

'Can you see any part of yourself as you float?'

After a long pause, 'No.' Then, again after a pause, 'I—can see myself in the *distance*! Floating down. It looks as though I'm going to come down and land on *me*!'

'Are you still in the same clothes?'

'I—I've got a vest. It's flapping in the wind. And I can *see* it flapping. Skinny ankles and long feet. I feel, I can *see* myself doing somersaults. I'm coming down. (Loud exhalation followed by a long pause.) It's getting black. He's coming down on top of *me*! I'm coming down on top of—no, I haven't. I've—landed...'

'What have you landed on?'

'I think it's going down on my *face*! With his *eyes* going down on my *face*! He seems to be just a small figure getting smaller and coming down on—my *face*!'

'Where are you now?'

'I'm lying down here.'

'You're back.'

'I'm here.'

'You're here in my room. It's all over.'

He opened his eyes, sat up, said he still had his dreadful headache and wanted something for it. He seldom got headaches, he said, but this was like 'seeing two motion pictures straight!' I gave him a codeine tablet and his headache was soon gone.

He was then asked if the experience had been vivid. He answered rather unexpectedly. 'When you asked me if the pavement was wet, I tried to *make* it wet, but it wouldn't.' He couldn't fake it, he said; he couldn't fake anything.

His head had been very heavy, right back here (he touched his occiput), whereas on marijuana he had always been light-headed. 'Even dizzy! You know—giddy!' Pot made him laugh a lot, especially Afghanistan 'shit', which was called 'shit' by the 'kids' not because it tasted like shit but because it looked like it. But it had never given him a headache like this had, nor made his head feel so heavy. On the other hand, pot had never given him any such experience like this either. 'Images, yes—but nothing at all like this.' He was absolutely intrigued with it. 'It leaves pot but for dead!'

'How long do you think you have been—there?'

'I'd say about—fifteen minutes.'

'You've been an hour and a quarter.'

'I haven't!'

And he immediately looked at his watch, disbelieved it, shook it at his ear, consulted it again, then looked incredulous. He even had to consult other watches while being assured by Ruby and Colin as well as Leo and me before he was convinced. I told him that with all that walking, he had exhausted us. He laughed, but then turned serious as he wondered at the denouement of his experience.

We wondered, too. Eventually we all seemed to agree that, probably because of some personal disaster as well as the catastrophe to the village, he had gone to the cliff-edge beyond the forest to jump—to commit suicide. Leo—quite ingeniously, I think—said that he himself felt at the time that Jim's headache and neck-pain was from an actual wound, probably sustained in whatever catastrophe had befallen the village. Anyway, Jim had jumped; and having jumped, he couldn't stop himself. His description of falling was much like that of many who have survived falling from great heights. There had been an account of one in the press only recently, of a youth who had jumped from a high bridge in Canada to evade the police, and who described the feeling as more like floating than falling, 'like a leaf in the wind, not at all like a stone'. Jim had not read this account. As so many do, Jim continued, he had appeared to lose consciousness while falling, only to find himself suddenly transposed into another body far below, watching his 'previous self'—which was all the time diminishing instead of increasing in size as he fell—falling towards him and then into him to disappear and thus end this rather long experience so dramatically.

I feel myself that his 'previous self', if that *is* what he was, had indeed committed suicide; and so his present mind, not wanting to experience the full fall and impact, had immediately switched back into his present self, perhaps as though his 'spirit' had indeed fallen from one body into another, and from one century into another. In which case, was the first descent to the Arc de Triomphe in Paris the mistake I had thought it at the time after all? 'The traffic would probably kill me,' he had said when asked to try to land there. Could this denote that he no longer had any suicidal tendency after the end of his 'previous life?' Why not? Indeed, he had seemed to shy away from the possibility most determinedly even at the beginning of such an 'experience' or dream as this.

Of course I am quite prepared for many, if not most, readers not to accept this explanation; but at least the experience does now convince me that, no matter what might befall the experimentee in his experience, it brings *no* harm to the present mind or body—otherwise Jim might be dead and Joy 'out of her mind'. So, frankly, at this point at least, I feel no apprehension any more in allowing experimentees to continue their experience, no matter how alarming it might become. The mind, or 'spirit', may be somewhere else—but the present body is very much *here*, in the present, where it belongs.

Two days after this experience of Jim McA—, on a wet afternoon, I made a second attempt with Leo, with just one other friend of ours in attendance to assist with the ankle-massaging.

This time Leo had much more success with all the preliminaries. His descriptions of the front door (of *my apartment* this time, instead of his home in Holland) and from the roof of the building here, were particularly graphic. The ascent was instant, for about ten kilometres, so I thought he was going to have success this time. Alas, not so.

When he descended again, on a brilliant day which at times was to become overcast with drizzling rain (it was overcast and drizzling outside), he could see only sunlit ocean and a ship. The ship was modern, he thought, but he couldn't be sure. After a while he could see land, but it was of the two northernmost tips of Australia (on either side of the Gulf of Carpentaria) from very high up. This, he said, he had once seen from an aeroplane when he was with the Dutch army in New Guinea nine years before. As he descended, the land and ocean became more like a map, spread flat on the surface of the earth, or on just an indeterminate surface. The ship had become absolutely stationary, including the smoke from its funnel. Try as he would, it remained that way, like a photograph. He could not go down any further.

So I took him up again and he tried once more. But now he merely saw a gap in the clouds, with some coastline and the same ship again. And again he said it was exactly like a photograph he had taken from the plane over New Guinea, with the one exception that he could see this in colour whereas the photograph was in black-and-white. Then the map-like land shifted north to include New Guinea, then even farther to Malaysia. Then, quite suddenly, it had 'whirled' to just over Scandinavia, but did not include Finland. But now he remained stationary—so did the map, till it darkened, dimmed, and disappeared.

Try as he would—and we tried for half an hour—he couldn't see anything. Nothing. He was quite sure the experiment wouldn't work for him even though he had witnessed so many successes, and however hard he might try. So, after half an hour, we stopped.

Talking it over, he decided that he felt the reason given for failures like this by the writer of the magazine *Open Mind* could apply to him—that he was reluctant and perhaps even afraid for the experiment to work with him because his 'previous life' had ended in violent death. I am not yet sure that I can accept this altogether, for I know that he had a rather unhappy and frustrating childhood and is often afraid to complete tasks, even simple domestic ones. Or, if not afraid, he simply doesn't finish them. However, I feel that a more likely reason is that he was being distracted by Joy's exuberance during the preliminaries of his first attempt, and in the second by the presence of a too-recent acquaintance.

The fault could also lie with me. Having taken so many people on these runs in the last ten days since returning from hospital, I could have been, if not impatient, then a little remiss with the instructions. Now I have read the *Open Mind* article again, and it says quite clearly that if the changing from day to night and back again is not accomplished easily then it must be repeated until it is. Further, I have so far made a point of not suggesting too much; but I see now that I should have told him, as advised, 'to keep the picture in bright sunshine—this is for two main reasons—firstly, so that when they land, they will be able to see where they are; and secondly by keeping the picture bright they are protecting themselves with light'.

I have resolved that on the next attempt with him, and with

others who do not appear to be succeeding, I shall have to be more explicit after all.

Leo also admits that, though he doesn't know why, he has instinctively been avoiding being an experimentee himself, to the extent of 'pushing other people into the experiment' whenever it had been arranged for him to undergo it. Again referring to the *Open Mind* article, one of the stipulations for the success of a run is that the experimentee should want to undergo it in order to experience 'a past life'. And Leo, so far, has been compulsively avoiding it.

Having assisted me with Leo and witnessed this failure, John M— said he wanted to try and so he and Leo changed places. He said he had been immediately intrigued and then impressed, although prior to that he had been most sceptical. He has just turned twenty-four and, having served two years' National Service with the army, with some of this time in Vietnam, he returned to Perth Technical College to complete the education he had abandoned before, though he is not yet sure how far he wants to go with education (to university or not) or what career he will choose. At the time of the experiment he was engaged to be married the next year. He is 5 ft 8½in. tall, weighs 10½ stone and has a good physique. With dark curly hair and hazel eyes, almost 'sculptured' lips and a very good complexion, he is very good-looking rather than handsome. He has a very pleasant personality and presence which has obviously been broadened by a trip to Europe. He is interested in music, art and literature, yet he is also athletic and keeps himself very fit.

He took twenty-two minutes over the preliminaries, which were all managed a little better than with most people, though he hadn't actually 'seen' the stretching and shrinking but merely 'felt' it. When he descended, he was over an ocean on a brilliant day, eventually approaching land that was not *quite* land as he seemed to see waves washing over it. But then these waves became smaller waves breaking on a shore which now he could see quite clearly, and on which he landed.

He could feel the fine warm sand under his bare feet which, when he studied them, he found to be brown, perhaps tanned or perhaps darker than his present skin, he wasn't sure. Looking up his legs, he said he was wearing nothing else but a brief 'lap-lap'. His whole body was very brown, all over, though whether this was from sun-bathing nude or was really his skin-colour, he still didn't know.

The sun was very warm on him and glinting on the beautiful ocean behind him and on the leaves of many palm trees before him. He thought the palms might have been coconutpalms but, as he thought he had never seen these, he wasn't sure. They had grey-green trunks going straight up, and he couldn't actually see any coconuts at the top. From this description I surmise that they were probably royal palms. They were very dense, he said, and came right down to the beach of this small and beautiful semi-circular lagoon enclosed by a reef. He felt he was on an island which looked tropical, a true paradise, a 'Utopia'; but he also felt sure that it wasn't tropical but warmly temperate. And the island was some way from land for it had taken him several days to get there by some kind of raft, or an outrigger, which he could see where he had left it on the beach.

He could also now see himself entirely. He had a roundish face with very dark eyes, a wide mouth, black bushy hair that was very thick, but he didn't seem to need to shave often, even though he thought, or felt, that he might be about forty. He was quite definitely of light brown pigment. He wasn't aware of having a name.

He was now walking into the palm forest which had beautiful undergrowth with 'lots of little yellow flowers and pink flowers' which he hadn't seen before; they were very flat flowers and very tiny, like miniature daisies. There was no path; he was just walking over grass about three inches high, very green. And now he had come to the other side of the palm forest and there was more water, very calm, of very deep colours, almost purple, and which he could now see was a small lake. The sun was much lower and was reflected here and there, so that he thought sunset was approaching.

Across the lake, on the opposite shore, was a small house on stilts, all thatched with wide open windows without any glass. But there were no doors. He could see right through the house as there were open windows on the other side of it as well. There were no people anywhere and no other houses, just this one. He was walking round the lake to it, and then saw that underneath there was a ladder leading up inside, a ladder made of grass rope.

Inside, he found himself in an area sunken two feet or so and about eight feet wide and even longer. The ladder led up into the middle of it and there was a trapdoor which he closed. This sunken area had a lot of animal skins or furs and was where he would sleep. A few steps led up to the rest of the house, or surrounding raised area. It was not a very big house, not much bigger than the sunken area, and was all very bare. It did have a big 'sort of sofa, a lounge-thing' at one side made of wood and skins. Over on the right, on the upper level, there were some small rough wooden chairs and a table. On the table was a bowl of fruit—oranges and bananas, with a little bunch of grapes—which made him feel all the more that, although the climate was beautifully warm, it wasn't tropical, for it had none of the sticky humidity of the tropics. It was—perfect. The bowl with the fruit was a shallow wooden bowl with a stem. The chairs, he could now see, 'had like—like—raffia on the seats' (he probably meant rattan). They were old, of a sort of 'bent wood'. There was a wooden cabinet with a hessian or raffia-type mat on the top. He didn't think there was anything else in the house.

He also didn't think that anyone else lived there, for it looked as though it hadn't been lived in for a long time. Yet he felt it had recently been made ready for him, and he was making himself at home in it. He had already closed the trapdoor in the centre of the sunken area and covered it over with the skins on which he would sleep. There was no one else on the island—no other man, or woman—and he didn't know who his predecessor might have been. 'Just—someone. Gone now.' Died? He didn't know. Who had prepared the house for him? He didn't know.

Just then a plane passed low overhead, rather noisily, so that it is very clear on the tape. But he didn't seem to register it. If he did, it didn't distract him at all.

Asked what he would do if he was hungry, he said he didn't know, but there was some kind of a stove in a fireplace which looked as though it hadn't been used for a long time, and even then might not have been used for cooking. He was much more explicit when asked what he would do if he wanted water. There was a sort of pipe made of woven raffia which you unhooked and, when lowered, the water ran out until you raised the pipe again and hooked it back. Where did the water come from? From a kind of vat-thing just outside, made of woven raffia or something like that. The water was very cool, probably from evaporation through the raffia covering.

He was now looking in the cupboard, but it was empty. There were no clothes or possessions of anyone else either in the cupboard or anywhere else in the hut. Asked who he thought had left the fruit there, he said he didn't know, because there was no one there. No animals? Some parrots, he could now see—very brightly coloured with reds and greens and yellows, and very long fine tails. They were flying around the house and sometimes perching on the window-ledge as though they were tame, or pets, or, for some reason, not afraid of him. And now there were also some monkeys, very small ones, which had jumped on to the window-ledge and were just sitting there watching him like pets. One was black and one was brown. He thought, now, that it had been these little monkeys which had picked the fruit and brought them to the bowl for him. It was as though they had known he was coming, and had prepared for him to the best of their ability.

Asked if he had changed at all now, he immediately said no. But then he said he could see that his hair wasn't quite as shaggy as it had been at first; and now, too, he seemed much younger, only about eighteen. As though to show him who had brought him the fruit, the monkeys had just put more in the bowl, he said—oranges and bananas.

Asked what he thought he was going to do, return or stay, he said he was going to stay there. He was never going to leave. This was why he had come—to get away from some place on land—or an island, several days across the sea—where his people lived absolutely meaningless and miserable lives, like robots, 'very busy'. He didn't think he had any parents, relatives or friends at all, but he couldn't be sure. All he knew was that he hadn't wanted to stay there any longer, or ever see it again, and so he had taken the raft-cum-outrigger and come alone over to this island, though whether he had previously known it to be there or not he also didn't know. He had—just come.

But now there was a zebra, and it was taking him somewhere around the island, he following it or walking at its side. He didn't at all attempt to mount it, as with a horse or donkey; it hadn't even occurred to him and he didn't even want to. He would walk. They had walked to one point of the island where the land was highest.

From here he could see that the island was sort of diamond-shaped—no, triangular. It was not very big, but it was very high in the middle. From where they were standing, the zebra and he, he could look straight down into the lagoon. Immediately below, at the foot of the precipitous cliffs, there were sharp rocks, about the only sharp rocks on the whole island. Looking further out, the lagoon in the sunset was brilliantly clear. He could see every ripple. And beneath the rippling surface he could clearly see the bottom, a kind of wavy sand, weeds, shells and other things.

The zebra? It was a sort of 'toy' zebra. Not toy in the sense of its being a toy, but small, with fur that was not hard like a horse's but cuddly and fluffy. Did the zebra have a name? He didn't think so. Did he have a name? He didn't know.

He was now going to the other side of the island, along the shore where there were very big rocks and pebbles; and shells, some very big shells. The whole island, small as it was, was exquisitely beautiful. Did he know where it was? He thought somewhere in the Pacific, but not in the tropics—somewhere where it was warm without being too warm. He thought it might be somewhere in the south of the Pacific. And here he was going to live, for the rest of his life.

He was going to build things—a waterwheel, to make power. Did he know how to get electricity from a waterwheel? No, but he would try to find out; he had seen it in the city from where he had come. But it didn't matter if he didn't succeed; he would merely try. The main thing he had to do was look after all the animals on the island, a lot of *little* animals...no, there was something like donkeys, and a baby elephant, lions and tigers, 'all playing together quite happily, as though they are still naked of any past experience. They don't fight with each other, let alone ever eat each other'.

He still didn't have a name, because he didn't need one. Nobody had a name because he was the only human and the animals didn't talk so they didn't need names, though they did listen to him when he talked to them and it seemed as though they understood him. Some were just single animals, just as he was the only human, and some had mates and could reproduce themselves. These latter would grow old and die, being replaced by their young. But those animals, and he himself, who were without a mate to reproduce with would live 'for ever' and not grow older after full maturity—then they, and he, would just stay as they were. It was like a small zoo, a Noah's Ark on an island, a paradise. 'There are no flies, or mosquitoes, or things like that. Only nice things. Nothing I don't like. No snakes—nothing nasty.'

He was still as he had been before, about eighteen, with light-brown skin all over, dark bushy straight hair that was bleached from the sun at the ends. He was a boy and not a girl, and he didn't have a girl; he had had one once, Marie, his fiancée, but she had chosen not to come with him when he had left the city to come to this island. He thought too, now, that he had also had parents, a family, but they were just like the 'robots' of the city, 'a kind of computerized people' leading their miserable lives, and he didn't want to see any of them again. He was sufficient unto himself; he didn't need anyone else. He was very happy on his island, the only human, but with all his animals.

None of them ate flesh, just fruit and vegetables (though he is not a vegetarian in real life). 'None of the animals have to kill each other; none of them have to live off each other.' There were not even fish to kill and eat, and no snakes. Whenever he lit a fire, by using a piece of glass and the sun, it was only to have warmth at night after the sun had gone down. He didn't cook anything—except maybe the corn he had planted when it grew. He had already used up his raft-cum-outrigger for firewood, and so he had no way of getting back even if he wanted to. He didn't want anyone with him; he was happy as though 'it was a great big game'.

He had made his waterwheel and it worked, but there was no power. Instead there was a little waterfall over which the stream dropped into the lagoon. 'I don't know what we use it for; it just looks nice.'

When asked if he had ever lived on such a paradise island, he said no, he had never been on it, but he would give anything to have such a place, to be able to 'stay there now'. He hadn't ever dreamt of it either. He was also still aware of being in my apartment and hearing the tape-recorder whirring and other occasional noises. These sounds he resented, and, almost as though to escape them, he said he was back up on the cliff where it formed a point, jutting out into the sea 'like the bows of a ship'. He talked again of the island and its inhabitants with a kind of wistful nostalgia. Then his voice began to adopt shades and nuances again—and quite suddenly, if most reluctantly, he was back. He was astounded when told that it had all taken an hour and a quarter exactly.

As most other experimentees, he wanted to talk about it all for some time, saying it was one of the most vivid and marvellous experiences he had ever known. At the same time he was quite practical about it. He didn't think it had been a 'past life' as much as something that might happen in the future, or else something of a 'dream-wish', something he deeply longed for as he didn't care much for most of the world the way it was. The length of the experiment had almost made him late for an appointment, but he telephoned the next morning to assure me again that 'none of the animals had been domesticated animals. None of them were used as beasts of burden, let alone to be killed and eaten.'

I wonder if he'll finish up as a vegetarian or a veterinarian, or both?

Author's note in August 1974: Shortly afterwards, John married a girl called Marie and is now completing three years' training to be a schoolteacher, so children will be his 'friendly animals'.

Chapter Eighteen

It seems that there might be some people after all for whom, unfortunately, this experiment does not work; and so they are deprived of a marvellous experience.

For the third time I attempted to run Leo under ideal conditions, with Ruby as my assistant. Again he managed all the preliminaries without difficulty. Indeed, on his third attempt, he was remarkably proficient and quick with them. But when it came to descending, even from what he said was a very great height, he would merely land right back on the spot where he had started.

Following *Open Mind*'s instructions, I had him change from day to night and back to day several times, then had him ascend again—only to have him land on a suburban beach a few miles away. Admittedly he had managed this on a bright sunny day, with crowds of other bathers around him, when it was actually a cool night, long before the swimming season started.

I then took him back through the stretching and shrinking exercises and all the rest of the preliminaries. But this time, instead of visualizing the front door of my apartment as we had just done twice already, I suddenly told him to visualize the door of a house in Amsterdam where he had been boarding when I first met him. He did this with more facility and, as I expected, he found the visualization exercise from a height above Amsterdam also easier to perform.

As might be expected, he landed on a coast which was obviously somewhere in the Netherlands, and more specifically on a dike, with the ocean, the North Sea, calm but dark on one side; on the other, fields of short young crops for the grazing of cows, but with these fields in fairly clear sunlight.

This dike, he said, stretched for miles; but he could see no villages, nor people, nor even grazing cows or sheep.

He couldn't even see himself. He wasn't standing on the asphalted narrow road of the dike, but was merely floating quite formlessly above it, at about the same height—almost six feet (one metre eighty)—as if he had been standing there. But he could still see nothing whatsoever of himself. Could he be a spirit? He didn't think so. Could he have some *other* form? He didn't know. Could he yet see anyone else or any*thing* else? 'No. But wait!'—he said. He *could*, if very dimly, see some windmills, very old ones, a short distance away. He was eventually able to 'drift' over to one and describe its paned windows and brown panelled door edged with glossy green paint. But he was unable to enter, nor could he tell if there was anyone inside. He felt uneasy, he said. He was quite sure that the experiment wouldn't work. 'Not with me.' He even *looked* apprehensive about it. Then he suddenly said everything had faded, and abruptly sat up.

However, I persevered. Since he was reluctant, and since I realized that he had been rather poor at visualizing from a height, I had him merely visualize an apple, a toy and several similar small objects; then I made him visualize the apartment above mine, which is familiar to him, then the last apartment above that, which is not familiar to him, then the roof and so took him aloft again.

But as soon as he was asked to descend—after more switching from day to night and back to day, and even though he could now see the required ocean and land far below the clouds in which he found himself—everything started to fade again, he said. It went either black or blank, and he was again apprehensive. So after having tried for over an hour with just these preliminaries, I grudgingly had to admit defeat with him yet once again.

He has said that he is willing to try again, but feels that the experiment won't work for him because he *does* have a reluctance to 'see whoever I might have been in the past, or where' as he had seen happen successfully with so many others. And he pointed out to me once again that the *Open Mind* article insisted that one pre-requisite for the experiment's success was for the experimentee to have a 'deep need' to see his or her possible past. So I have decided that if he is to be run again it will only be when he himself comes to me and says he feels ready and *wants* to try once more—if only because his reluctance is due, perhaps, and as he suspected, to his having been blind in some possible past life.

In contrast with Leo's third run and his having had plenty of time for preparation, let alone having witnessed so many previous experimentees, the following two had all too little preparation or even explanation, due to the brief time available and the pressure of their work. In the latter respect, both are highly qualified professionals following university education in very practical fields.

David H— is a twenty-four-year-old unmarried geologist from Melbourne who, when not in the field, in the hot and desolate far north or outback of Western Australia, has a room in the apartment of Colin N—, through whom he had heard of the experiment. He was curious to try it, after a little further clarification about it.

He is probably one of the most highly qualified experimentees I have had. One of his passions is painting, at which he is proficient and imaginative. I have four of his ink drawings which please me very much.

The experiment took place in my apartment on Sunday, September 12th, with Colin, Ruby and Leo also present. David's preliminaries were adeptly performed, especially the visualizing exercises from in front of the door and on top of the roof of Colin N—'s apartment building.

He descended on a bright sunny day over sea—and *only* sea—that was calm and of a grey-green colour. He thought he was in a small aeroplane somewhere 'northish' as he was dressed in only a lightweight grey suit without shirt or underclothes or even shoes and socks. He was descending quite rapidly now. Yes, he thought he was going to land on the water. No, it wasn't a seaplane. He thought he was the only one in it but he wasn't sure, he was too concerned and too busy looking where he was going to land. Then, he said, he had hit the sea and *passed under it*. He then remained silent, and very still, for quite a long time.

When I asked him what he was doing now, he said he was lying washed up on a beach. He was still wearing the same grey suit without anything else. He was lying prostrate with his face on coarse sand, his body half in and half out of the water which he could feel washing coolly over him. He couldn't move; he couldn't move at all.

But wait! He thought he could see himself emerging from *out* of himself as he lay there, leaving his prostrate figure, but now in another 'kind of figure' that was absolutely stiff, with his hands at his sides, and with his feet sticking out at right-angles from his legs 'like Charlie Chaplin'. He could see along the beach to either side as well as beyond it, because he was now seeing from a normal height instead of having his face flat on the sand. Yet he wasn't walking along or over the beach; he was *floating* over it, still stiff, and with his hands at his sides and his feet in this ludicrous and incredible position. He was also still in his damp grey suit.

He wandered inland over country that, he soon recognized, was much like that around Shark Bay and more specifically Hamelin Pool (about five hundred miles north of Perth, but also just as far south-west of his usual locality at Marble Bar) and which he had once seen in actuality. He could see some 'dirty' sheep and lambs with long tails, and an occasional fence, but no habitation or people or other animals. He was 'following' a double track made by some kind of vehicle, yet there was none in sight. He was still floating rather than walking, and he could see the countryside in brilliantly sharp sunshine in detail.

It seemed to the rest of us that he floated for mile upon mile, for hours! He followed this rough two-wheeler track which had just been worn into the bare dry earth, with nothing around but low parched scrub. There were no habitations and no people. It even took him some time to see more animals, three kangaroos. Then, quite unexpectedly, the three kangaroos suddenly split up to go in different directions. One was very young, what is called a 'joey'. It suddenly ran directly towards him and, as they quite frequently do, leapt up into his arms. He *felt* its impact and warmth, its fur. The mother kangaroo, seeing what had happened, stopped and watched for a few moments while the father still ran his own way. Then, too, the mother loped off again. The joey snuggled into him as he floated off above the earth. Then, to his consternation, he found himself floating higher and higher above the earth, so that it would be fatal if the joey should fall. To prevent this, he tucked it inside his suit coat and against his body, feeling its fur and warmth to an even greater extent. The mother and father had disappeared, so he continued on his way with the joey snuggling into him, and occasionally stretching up to sniff at David's nose.

Again, still with the joey inside his coat, he floated for mile upon mile—until he came to a small hut in the middle of an arid and deserted landscape. At first he thought there was no one there, until he looked at a near-by hill and saw that there was an entrance to a small tunnel-like mine there in the hill's talus. Narrow rail-tracks emerged from it. Soon a man of about fifty-five emerged, pushing a wheeled bin on the tracks. So *he* was the miner, a man David knew in real life but not very well, and not in these particular circumstances or surroundings. Then he could also see a youth—a rather moronic specimen, he said, of about eighteen. He knew then what he must do; he descended and gave the joey to them. As he floated away again, the man laughed uncontrollably; but the youth merely gaped in astonishment. The man had not been surprised at seeing another man flying, but the youth was dumbfounded.

On he went again, still in the same unusual attire and absurd attitude, floating or flying across the entire desert-type centre of Australia—with its salt-lakes and mountain ranges and great droves of cattle—until he found himself approaching 'quite a big town near Canberra called Yass' (approximate population is almost four thousand), which he recognized by an overhead bridge. He didn't want to land there—indeed he couldn't land anywhere—but merely wanted to float over the town with its people and traffic. He came very close to one middle-aged woman with an enormous red nose and saw several aboriginals standing or lounging around. He could see every building and house and vehicle as though he was indeed there in reality. But then he had passed over it and was on his way.

He knew he wasn't a bird flying about like this; so, as he could see himself in this absurdly stiff attitude all the time, he presumed himself to be some kind of 'spirit' of himself. He might even have died, and his 'soul' or 'spirit' was rushing across the entire continent towards where, in reality, he had been born and brought up as a child.

During his long and amazing journey, he described the land beneath him in both an ordinary person's and a geologist's terms; and, of course, he knew the country extremely well. But in order to précis the account of this long journey of his—from day to night and back to day again, under various and varying skies, feeling alternately hot and cold—I have omitted by far the greater part of the incredible detail he supplied to us as he flew over 'country going on for ages', still in his same grey suit with light buttons which was now, like himself, very dirty, he said.

Yes, he could hear various sounds in the room, especially the whispering whirr of the tape-recorder and remote traffic-sounds. The mention of this made him aware of his actual presence in the room, and for a moment I thought he was back. He very nearly was. Yet he was still partially 'there' as well, again seeing aboriginals. He could have gone on for ages, he said, although he didn't know where he was going and in any case he didn't think he was going anywhere in particular. He was just 'going'. 'But when I go, I go like a rocket!'

Then he said he thought he might fly over to his home eventually, although he wouldn't stay or even land there. He'd just 'see it', then go on, aimlessly, he thought for 'all time' unless he stopped the experience now.

And so he did, astounded that the hour and twenty-five minutes he had taken wasn't just the five minutes he had thought. He agreed that he hadn't glimpsed any past life. On the contrary, he thought it 'might have been a bit in the future'. Was there any point to it? He didn't know. If there were, it might be just a warning not to fly in any amateur pilot's small plane, especially over the sea, as he quite frequently did. No, he had never dreamt any of this; but he did find it a *bit* like 'day-dreaming', except that *this* was both so very real and so vivid in both form and colours. Landscapes, he said, had seemed even more sharply real than in reality, perspectives surrealistic.

He said he hadn't been at all influenced into seeing what he had, nor had he influenced himself into seeing it. And he most certainly couldn't have 'faked' any of it, he averred. For the entire time since being washed up on the beach, he felt that he 'had been looking at the world from the outside'. He very much wanted to 'do' it again—and try to see something of the past next time.

Paul L—, thirty-eight and unmarried, was born amongst

various races in Malaysia, and more specifically in Kuala Lumpur where he completed his primary and secondary education, coming to Adelaide in South Australia for his long tertiary education to qualify for his present profession of orthodentist with his own practice. He is of slight build with black hair and dark brown eyes, very full and precisely shaped lips, and an appearance that would be good-looking to most people. He has the strong yet agile hands required by his profession.

Paul's experiment was performed in his own surgery early in a mild but overcast and showery September evening. He used his Italian dental couch, which adjusted to enable patients to be moved from sitting-up, through various positions of leaning, to lying at full length! At first I was a little apprehensive of the severity of the overhead fluorescent lights and I still think these were responsible for the restricted range of his experience. Had I thought of it at the time, 'piped' music which he used to soothe patients was available, and at a suitably low volume. Perhaps next time.

Paul—if not genuinely interested in the experiment, then at least curious—performed the preliminaries with almost amazing alacrity, though he admitted that he couldn't actually *see* his feet or head in the exercises for the 'elasticizing' of the body but could merely *feel* them. Yet he could clearly see his front door of the duplex home he owns, and also the surroundings from the roof. But difficulties now began with the ascending despite the fact that he travelled round the world by plane, for his practical mind boggled at such an *im*practical suggestion.

However, once having ascended by being exhorted to 'imagine' he had attained the required height, he could then see quite widely and clearly. But when asked to change from day to night, everything he saw merely went 'black'. He could see nothing. There were neither lights below nor stars above. Not even a moon. Restoring the scene to daylight, all was as previously, and the day clear and sunny. When asked, he said it was indeed he himself who was doing the changing but at my 'instruction' to do so. We tried several times, till eventually he did see lights but only from a fairly low level, and it was again difficult to have him ascend again. If he did, he merely landed in the city of Perth.

Eventually he could see himself approaching the American continent, both north and south, and found himself descending towards the Central American isthmus and more specifically the Panama Canal, which he has never in reality seen nor even been near. He landed at the concrete side of the canal near a small building where two coloured men were working, although there were no ships visible in the canal. He could visualize a lock to the left with the lower level of water beyond it. To the right, the canal wound away inland at the same level as before him through dense tropical trees of an indeterminate nature. He didn't want to enter the building because of the excruciating noise from the machinery, in contrast with his surgery room which was particularly quiet despite its location near a very busy intersection of the city. But he could still detect the occasional and actual slight noise around him. He spent some time at the canal, but saw himself only as he was at present and didn't think there was anything in particular he wanted or needed to see or do. So I had him ascend again—into dense cloud! When he had passed through the cloud's density and dimness, even darkness, it was 'pretty bright' above.

Further descents brought him down to local places not very distant from Perth and in the present time, and even as he had seen them on recent visits. The noise from the machinery at the Panama Canal had long since stopped, he said. Numerous ascents and descents had to be tried, till finally he did at least arrive somewhere else by using the artifice of an old-fashioned 'balloon'. He found himself descending towards snow-peaked mountains.

When he landed, he stepped out of the balloon's basket but 'didn't like it' because he had stepped out on to a rough gravel road of sharp stones which 'hurt his feet with only his socks on'. He was still himself, and still in the present. I wanted him to try ascending just once more before abandoning the experiment but he didn't want to, he was enjoying himself so much just looking at the beautiful scenery. The snow-capped mountains reared to his right while a valley lunged down to his left, almost completely covered with grass about twelve inches high. Far below there was a lone farmhouse, very small, with some sheep round it. It had a brown door, small windows, red roof and light grey walls of rough-hewn stones. He could see no people at all and there wasn't even smoke coming from the chimney.

There were no outhouses or other buildings or even animals around, and he had never seen the place before.

He followed the rough gravel path only when he had obtained 'some rough suede-leather boots from the balloon's basket so that he could walk'. And so he walked. He walked and walked until Leo and I were almost exhausted from it, much as he enchanted us with his descriptions of mountains and the curving ascent of the road—till eventually he had gone as high as he could go. Yes, it was indeed cold, but 'only up *there* and not down *here* where I really am'. There was nothing else to do, though he was quite happy just to stay there indefinitely, looking at all this magnificent landscape which, he said, could have been in Norway yet was perhaps in New Zealand.

There seemed little point in his landscape-gazing, so I had him ascend again. More snow-capped mountains! But this time he said they were in Tasmania where he had practised for a few years after graduating and before coming to Perth.

Up once more, then down again—to more mountains! But this time he said he was descending to the courtyard or square of a 'small village like Salzburg' (no, he hadn't read Jim McA— nor any of the MS so far). Yet it wasn't Salzburg because it was much too small. Perhaps Innsbruck? No, smaller than that. Two-storey buildings surrounded him, a church with a spire and other more elaborate buildings, the snow-capped mountains quite clear beyond. There were precisely four men in the square; they were dressed in 'lederhosen' and white shirts with braces, boots with socks and high-peaked caps. But he didn't want to stay here; he wanted to go to the mountains. So he left the village and followed yet another rough gravel path. He still wore his same 'desert boots' and present clothes, and was therefore still himself.

The path led him to fields of rich and tallish green grass with flowers here and there. But there were few if any trees, just low bushes. The mountains always called him. He wanted to be in the snow. Yet try as he would—and walk as *far* as he would—he never seemed to get beyond a small stream rippling over round stones, the water of which was very cool, almost chilled, but tasted marvellous. He was again cold there; but not 'here', in his room. He wanted nothing else but to go on to the mountains.

But then, to his amazement—and this feeling was very clear

in actuality on his face and with the sudden raising of his arms with hands outspread—he realized that he couldn't find his way. What would he do? What *could* he do? Return to the village and find one of the men there who would be able to tell him. So he did this, with remarkable speed, and soon found, of the four men, one who 'automatically understood him, though perhaps he did speak English too', and who said that, Yes, he did know the way and would show it to him. They set out together, along the same gravel road and through the same fields and tall green grass—then came to an abrupt halt at the very same stream.

There was now consternation on Paul's face. Again his hands rose into mid-air, then stopped there. Yet his feet crossed and then scratched and scratched at themselves while he just gaped with such anguish that I was tempted to bring him out of the experience, or at least remind him that it was all just a dream, if a conscious one, and that in any case he himself could terminate it at any time. But then Paul suddenly said, 'My God! He doesn't know! He doesn't know! So I might as—well go *back...*'

And he was back. It had been an hour and a quarter of, to him at least, enthralling armchair (or surgery-couch?) travelling in brilliant colour and explicit detail; but I myself could see little point in further attempts with Paul. We were all convinced that the forethought especially, and then the preliminaries, had been much too brief and hasty in his case, requiring tiresome repetitions of ascents and descents. Yet Paul was surprised that he had managed to see anything whatsoever as he said he was not at all given to 'daydreaming', unless one included contemplation of his work; he was not at all imaginative and did not even recall dreams—*if* he dreamt at all. He thought that his intense preoccupation with his work precluded him from indulging in very much else, even sport or hobbies for relaxation, let alone any form of 'astral travel'. He had guessed the actual time of his 'trip' from Panama onwards almost to the minute. And that, we thought, was that.

But not so; he then said that he found the whole matter 'very interesting'. The situation, he continued, applied precisely to his work at the present time. He had reached a stage, he said, when to improve his methods and so arrive at the 'peak' of his profession (and consequently provide himself with the pleasant surroundings he craved?) he had come to a 'stumbling-block', a 'full-stop'. He had been considering going to the university where he had learnt his profession, or to a highly specialized colleague. 'But this shows it will be of no use,' he said. 'I will just have to find the way myself.'

He was booked to fly to New Zealand for a brief and much needed holiday the following Friday, after which he would consult or inquire from his colleague as soon as possible. But for now? Now, he said, he would have to consider the experience and its possibilities from a much more serious approach, just in case it could be of assistance.

There is a further surprising element in his merely having seen mountain landscapes that could have been in Norway or New Zealand, with one indeed located in Tasmania, though his first visit to the Panama Canal was probably just as surprising. I had expected him, if he had seen any past life at all, to have gone at least to somewhere in Asia, most likely to China. For Paul is of pure Chinese blood.

Author's note in August 1974: Paul married his English assistant in 1973 and during their eight-week honeymoon in Europe they visited Norway, and saw the exact scene he had described in his Christos Experience – a village surrounded by mountains which he had thought to be in either Norway or New Zealand. To show me, he photographed this small village in Norway's rugged and mountainous north near Andalnes. While in London, he consulted professional colleagues, only to find them to be no further advanced than he; with his wife's assistance, he is now conducting his own research here in Perth.

Chapter Nineteen

THE PROCEDURE

First Stage

The experimentee, or person being 'run', is to lie flat on his back on the floor with a cushion under his head and with his shoes off. Socks or stockings can be left on.

With his eyes firmly closed, the person's ankles are massaged for two or three minutes to 'loosen' them and induce relaxation.

Shortly after starting to massage the ankles, another person (usually the one doing the running, i.e. the suggesting and questioning) massages the 'third eye' position, or lower centre of the forehead between the frontal lobes of the brain, in a circular motion with *the edge of his curved hand*, so that it fits snugly into this 'third eye' position or cavity. The massaging should be vigorous rubbing, till the experimentee feels his head really buzzing.

The experimentee must be fully relaxed. If he is still a little tense, he should take several deep breaths and then let himself go limp.

Second Stage

Now commence the mental exercises to make the relaxed experimentee expand his mind beyond its normal limits in his physical body. It doesn't matter if the person is spiritually 'aware' or not, the technique still works. But of course the greater the sense of 'spiritual awareness' the person has, the greater will be his ability to see and understand his experience. Also, *Open Mind* states that a deep inner need to find out something of a past life is necessary to provide it, which may explain the failure of those experimentees to see nothing more than a rather ordinary dream sequence.

The person is then asked to *visualize his own feet* as he lies there with his eyes still closed until the experiment is over.

Then he is asked to visualize himself *growing two inches* (or five centimetres) taller (or 'longer', being horizontal), through the bottoms of his *feet.* He just has to *feel* himself two inches taller, but some will actually *see* it happen at the ankles.

He is then asked to say when he is two inches taller, the person doing the instructing waiting till he has done so. At this stage, the experimentee should be encouraged to start talking as much as possible, so that he will become accustomed to the idea for later on when it is very necessary for him to describe his experience.

Once he has 'stretched' two inches, he is asked to *return to his normal length* or height, trying to see or feel (or both) his feet returning towards him to their normal position.

Repeat this several times till he becomes accustomed to the process, always waiting for each stretch and return to be accomplished.

Now repeat the entire process, but *through his head.*

Then return to *the feet* and have him stretch and return them a distance of *12 inches* (20 centimetres).

Repeat the same distance through his *head.*

Again return him to his feet and have him stretch and return *24 inches* (40 centimetres). The instructor can tell if the person is having difficulty as this 24-inch or 40-centimetre stretch should be accomplished in under a minute. Have the experimentee repeat till he does so.

DO NOT have him return from this longest stretch, but have him stretch the same distance, 24 inches (40 centimetres) *through the head.* If he says he finds his feet are withdrawing as he stretches through his head, have patience and persevere until he has accomplished stretching in both directions.

While stretched 4 feet (80 centimetres), ask him next to *expand* all over, to feel himself growing in all directions, rather like an enormous balloon. This expands him 'out' of himself. The next step is to start him seeing things—familiar things at first—so he is now to picture himself as he normally is, but standing outside his own front door.

Third Stage

Ask him to look at his own *front door* and describe it to you in full. Ply him with as many questions as you can about it until he has fully described the door *and* its surroundings, including what he is standing on and what is above him when he looks up.

Once he has managed to look at his front door with what is called 'expanded consciousness', he must then become accustomed to a feeling of free movement while obtaining a much wider range of 'vision', or visualizing. You now ask him to imagine he is standing *on the top of his roof* and to describe what his garden or immediate surroundings look like from that height. Keep on asking for details as this makes him accustomed to 'seeing' without the use of his actual eyes.

Now ask him to *go straight up in the air about 500 yards* (or 500 metres will do just as well) and to keep talking as he looks down, describing all he can now see from this greatly increased height. If he should baulk at the height, remind him that he is still actually on the floor and is only *visualizing* being at that height.

Now ask him to *turn slowly in a complete circle* and describe everything he sees, to accustom him to seeing from an unnatural viewpoint.

This done, *ask what time of day it is* while he is seeing what he is. Usually it is daytime, but it can be at various times and with very different weather; yet neither time nor weather will be related to actual conditions.

Now, if he is seeing during the day, ask him to *change the scene to night-time*, and to describe all he sees as it now is.

Then ask him to *change back to daytime* and to compare the scene with how it was at night-time. It doesn't matter if they differ, but they are usually the same.

Next, to give him assurance of safety for the remainder of the experiment, *ask who is changing from day to night and back to day again*. Most will say '*I* am', or '*I* am, but at *your* suggestion.' It is very important that he realizes that he himself has the control over whatever he is seeing.

Fourth (and vital) Stage

If you are satisfied that the person is content in his newly expanded environment, you now carefully guide him to the experience—and possibly to a past life.

Tell him, rather than just ask him, to *keep the picture in bright sunshine* so that he can see clearly where he *lands, feet first.*

While looking down he should see his feet, so you have him commence his description of wherever he finds himself by *describing his feet*, if bare, or what he is wearing on them (often shoes, though of course in reality he is wearing socks or is barefooted from the preliminary massaging).

Go on from the feet to ask him *what kind of ground* he is standing on.

Then ask him to *look around* him a little.

If he is in, say, a courtyard, ask *what kind of buildings*, etc., are round him.

Are there *other people* there, or not?

Can he see *what else he is wearing*?

Can he see *his hands*, and what is on them?

Can he see his *face*? His *features*? His *figure* as a whole?

(N.B. As in dreams, most subjects can 'go outside' their bodies and look at them quite objectively.)

Is he *standing still*, or now *walking*?

Keep pressing for details until he is firmly 'locked in' on whatever environment he now finds himself in. If in a marketplace, can he see a fruit-stall? What kind of fruit is on it? How much fruit? Keep questioning him till he either tires of it or else he sees clearly and sharply, and in vivid colour, if he isn't already doing so.

Watch the eyelids for rapid eye and eye-muscle movements. The faster the rate of the flicker, the more successful is the vision or dream.

And from now on you must literally *play it by ear.* Try not to ask suggestible questions but merely ask what he is seeing or doing, then follow up with relevant questions such as, 'Colour?' 'What do you feel?' 'How old is he?' 'What is she wearing?' 'Do they speak to you?' 'In what language, or do you just "understand"?'

Try to have a *tape-recorder* going from when he *lands* so that further details can be asked about the experience after it is over.

After a while, usually about three-quarters of an hour, he may say he has seen all he wants to; or, if he has become quiet, you must ask him if he *has* seen all that he wants to. If he says yes, you can then ask him if he wants to go on to the *experience of death*, or return directly to everyday life. He is *not* in a trance, but is absolutely conscious to choose what he likes. It is merely a matter of re-locating his consciousness to return to the present. He should at *any* time, if asked, be able to identify sounds around him *in the present* while still seeing his past life or experience.

He himself is able to return, or stop the experience, at any time he wishes. However, as in an actual dream, an experimentee usually does not wish to terminate it until it has come to a logical conclusion, and even then he is sometimes quite reluctant to return to the humdrum reality of the present compared with what he has just been experiencing—unless he is impatient to talk about it.

Keep an account of *the time* taken. Usually the preliminary procedure takes about twenty minutes, while the experience itself takes anything from half an hour to over an hour, as with an ordinary dream, so that the entire process should take an hour or more. Usually the experimentee will think he has 'been away' for only a quarter of the time and will be astonished at just how long the experience lasted.

Chapter Twenty

Man's earliest book or record of his dreams and his interpretations of them dates back to around 1350 B.C., and so is more than 3,000 years old. It is known as the 'Chester Beatty papyrus', named after the man who donated it to the British Museum. The 'dream book' itself comes from the early Egyptians. It contains about two hundred dreams and their interpretations, divided into 'favourable' and 'unfavourable' ones—which makes my recording of only twenty-four dreams, *without* much in the way of interpretation, a fairly modest number after all. Certainly they may seem too many if you have chosen to read this book merely for entertainment value, like a novel. But on the other hand they may be too few if their purpose is to be a documentary record.

However, for my present purposes I think there are enough. I could go on experimenting endlessly, and I still have a number of 'special' people with whom I would like to try the experience. But for this present book I think there are now sufficient examples and details to show that—whatever might have been claimed for the experiment in the first place—something very extraordinary does indeed happen, a phenomenon which leaves me astounded at its not having been discovered long ago.

I shall be even more astounded should I learn that it has indeed been discovered in various parts of the world, yet has still not become 'common knowledge' to people everywhere.

Then again, perhaps the psychology of the world population is only just emerging into the phase where such a phenomenon (like extra-sensory perception and other allied phenomena) can be accepted. Or perhaps previous experimenters either did not have the full preliminary procedure, or else were seeking only revelations of past experiences. And this, we have seen all too clearly, does not always happen. But what does happen is still marvel—even miracle—enough.

Conscious or 'Day' Dreams?

Even if all that happens is no more than a dream under conscious control (yet more than a daydream), this would be marvel enough: most of us are not aware of just how much we do dream in our sleep, as has been proved by scientific experimentation.

And though we may happen to be aware of dreams, almost invariably we are frustrated by not being able to remember them upon waking, not even *immediately* upon waking. Science shows that we remember only a small fraction of our dreams, just as conscious memory retains only a fraction of all our conscious experience, the vast majority being consigned to and retained by the subconscious, from which it can be 'resurrected' by various methods used in modern psychiatry, mostly involving the use of drugs, hypnotism, electronic equipment or lengthy psychiatric consultations.

Perhaps this method which provides the recipient with such vivid dreams or experiences, merely trips the release mechanism of our source of dreams. This source is said by most scientists to be situated at the back and base of the brain, below and just inside the occiput.

The preliminary massaging of the forehead might seem to some to have little bearing on this other part of the head, until one considers that mental activity is an enormous system of minute electrical currents in the chemical 'environment' of the brain. Consequently, massaging, like the rubbing of a magnet, could and no doubt does stimulate these currents into many activities which are, perhaps, normally neglected. At the same time, the massaging of the forehead particularly in the 'third eye' position between and just above the two actual eyes, automatically applies a certain amount of pressure, and also movement, to the back of the head, especially to that part of it just below the occiput which rests on the cushion.

The simultaneous massaging of the ankles most certainly 'decentralizes' one's consciousness of being massaged, for most minds fly from one extremity of the body being massaged to the other, instead of remaining static and therefore somewhat soporific when massage is applied, as it mostly is, to only one location of the body at a time. This simultaneous but very different massaging, performed by two people, can be likened to that maddening children's game of endeavouring to rub the stomach with a circular motion with one hand while vertically raising and lowering the other above the head.

More than just for mere relaxation before the rest of the experiment, this simple massaging obviously also releases the mind from its normally rigid confinement within the severe limitations of purely practical and utilitarian, even materialistic, matters. This release prepares the way for the elementary visualization exercises which immediately ensue.

These exercises follow an obvious, logical progress towards attaining the conscious dream, from the elasticizing and expansion of the body, to freeing the mind from its normally rigid physical confinement, to commencing to 'see', by means of memory, familiar surroundings first near, then far, then blending these with increasingly imaginative visualization during the ascent. At the zenith of this ascent, the mind becomes free from both its own limitations as well as those of the body, both of which normally confine the activity or conceptions of the brain itself. And so the experience begins in much the same way, I have come to believe, as a normal dream would begin were the experimentee to be asleep. But, of course, he isn't asleep; he is wide awake—even 'wider' awake, if one may refer literally to that cliché, than is usual for the great majority of people. In other words, he is now consciously receptive to his subconscious without the normal requisite of sleep.

Even the 'trips' attained while under the influence of LSD 25 and other psychedelic drugs are considered by some psychologists as mere extensions (however great these extensions may be) in the length of dream-time in sleep. People under the influence of such drugs cannot be awakened; they are not simultaneously aware of their experience and their physical surroundings, nor can they bring themselves back to the actual world should they want to. Not only are all these things possible in the Christos Experiment, but also the experimentee can recount what is happening as he experiences it. Furthermore, Richard B— said he found the Christos Experiment to be much more vivid, realistic, meaningful and even 'entertaining' than taking LSD.

The effects of marijuana, according to Jim McA— (Chapter 17) and several others I have asked, are more a sense of physical and psychological well-being or euphoria, in which images or visions fleetingly, if sometimes vividly, appear. But at the most these visions only approach those much more 'heightened' images induced by the drug mescalin which the late Aldous Huxley experienced and commended in his *Doors of Perception.* We have, so far, only Jim McA—'s word that his Christos experience was so much more than any he had known with various kinds of marijuana.

Both LSD and marijuana have detrimental physical effects on the body; admittedly, those of marijuana are minimal compared with LSD, and, over long periods, they are also much less harmful than those of cigarettes and alcohol—the socially tolerated drugs which have become two of the world's biggest industries.

So if the Christos Experiment can provide humanity with an inner revelation it is now so obviously seeking, and which it is so very justified in seeking (indeed, perhaps the one mystifying aspect to this psychological phenomenon only so recently appearing in man, at least as a 'mass movement', is that it has taken so *long* to become manifest), then the use of this simple procedure will be of tremendous benefit to mankind, for it involves none of the physical damage already being suffered by so many people—many of them very young—from drugs of varying potency.

Dreams of Psychological Significance?

Even Leo had an elementary form of a conscious dream in the first of his attempts (when he returned to the Netherlands in Chapter 5), however fruitless it may have seemed; and in his second and third attempts he went some way towards achieving it. Such dreams were experienced by Stephan M— (in Chapter 9), vividly by David K— (when he flew in Chapter 10), by Colin N— (in the first part of Chapter 16), by David H— (when he flew with the baby kangaroo in the second part of Chapter 18) and also by Paul L— (when he mountaineered in the third part of Chapter 18).

None of these experiences could be said to be revelations of past lives as claimed in the *Open Mind* magazine, but some of them at least do indicate something rather more than a series of meaningless images.

I think this is certainly so with Geoffrey W— and his surrealistic well which became first a cave and then an open-cut mine from which he could emerge as either boy or man (in Chapter 16). He feels, and his wife feels very strongly, that the experience pointed to his present stage of leaving childhood and youth to face the responsibilities of adulthood, in his case as a school-teacher. I have no doubt that a psychiatrist would find the account of his 'dream' of great significance, probably as a sign that he should accept the necessity of evolving into adulthood.

Something similar can also be said for Colin N— (in Chapter 16) and his three locales of isolation and loneliness. Indeed, it was he himself who remarked on this.

Paul L—'s ostensibly very elementary visits to mountainous locales (in the third part of Chapter 18) culminated in something much more meaningful and he himself saw in the experience an allegory for his work.

John M—'s paradise island with all the young animals (in the third part of Chapter 17), is another case of an experience being of considerable psychological help, for in a list which I have consulted of dream symbols as interpreted by modern psychoanalysts (for example, kings and queens being interpreted as the dreamer's parents, a bridge being a way of overcoming an obstacle, a river being a turning-point in one's life), it states that 'small animals may stand for children'. And John M— was facing the decision between taking up a career of medical technology (laboratory work) or school-teaching, both of which involved the same duration of time (six years) and expense. According to this interpretation of his experience, the school-teaching should be his choice. I hope it is; his charming personality and kindness and patience with children would be wasted in a laboratory.

David B—'s glimpse of himself in a possible but very recent past near a small Queensland outback town, where he lived with his dog in a small hut (Chapter 11) was, to him, an indication not to follow the career set out before him, of some legal capacity in a big city, which would be psychologically unsuitable for him.

Peter C—'s revelation (in Chapter 12, which took place under most unsuitable conditions) of an actual past incident in his present life, when he was, however, a child of only three, explained to him, he said afterwards, his fear of water; having thought about his 'revelation' for several weeks, he said he suddenly realized that what had upset him at the time was someone trying to entice him into the water, even though he still didn't know who that someone might have been, and that it had taken some considerable time and will-power to overcome his aquaphobia.

Precisely the same job of discovering, interpreting and explaining a problem of psychological disturbance is done by a psychoanalyst or psychiatrist; but this is usually accomplished with lengthy consultations, which often involve reference to dreams that are poorly or barely remembered. If this Christos method is capable of producing exactly the same result while one is conscious and able to recount every detail of the dream or revelation as it is actually occurring, it should be of enormous value and assistance to this new science. That would be an even greater marvel than the mere use of it as some novel form of entertainment.

Dreams of Prediction?

But now there are three of the twenty-four experiences which contained another element, the first of which was the last part of Stephan M—'s experience (in Chapter 9) when, he was quite convinced, he was transported approximately three years into the future, specifically to his mother's funeral. Is this a literal prediction? There are many spiritualists and believers in clairvoyance and extra-sensory perception who readily declare that it can be. Yet on the other hand there are very many more sceptics and those who *immediately* discount such possibilities or who will not even give them consideration.

Attitudes towards such matters have been changing in recent years, resulting, perhaps, from the population explosion which has created a vast and rapidly expanding 'mass psychology' both of and for humanity. Consequently, there are now scientists, such as mathematicians, who are ready to concede, or who have indeed already suggested, that our impression of time, for instance, is not accurate. Instead of the line of continuum from past through present to future, time could be a dimension much like that of length and width simultaneously, or even three-dimensional in itself. In that case, what has already happened might still exist, and what has not yet happened has already been here. Events could appear to happen merely because we ourselves move along a dimension of time, and events could seem to happen *in sequence* because we have an awareness of that dimension of time. Without it, everything—and therefore nothing—would happen at once.

Impressions from the subconscious mind seem to indicate this possibly wider, or more expanded, dimension of time; for to the subsconscious things may happen as though there is no time, no possibility of these things happening when we are conscious, or awake. So perhaps a glimpse of the future, so often provided by *predictive* dreams which are now accepted by psychologists, is not impossible. Why should it be impossible when we know there are such things as predictive subconscious dreams, particularly the famous one of Abraham Lincoln in which he saw himself just before his assassination? In the dream he was 'walking from room to room in the White House, hearing people crying although he was unable to see anyone until he walked into the East Room, and then saw soldiers guarding a coffin while a crowd of people were weeping; and when he inquired who was dead in the White House, he was told "The President. He was assassinated" '. And a few days later he *was* assassinated by the actor, John Wilkes Booth.

But yet—the interpretation of dreams of death given by the early Egyptians (according to the Chester Beatty papyrus) is that the person seen dying or dead will have a long life; but that interpretation was given 3,000 years ago. Today it would, more than likely, be accepted in a much more literal or even predictive sense. But at the same time it is 'a long journey' which is mostly associated with death and/or the idea of going on to another plane or existence. Catching a train or a plane in a dream can also denote the possibility of death, while missing one can suggest an escape from it or its postponement.

Three years must pass before the prediction of Stephan M—'s vision of his mother's funeral (in Chapter 9), can be proved. Undoubtedly it explains his reluctance at the time to try the experiment again, although he has since expressed a change of mind about that. His excuse? He thought the dream might have been a message to him to adopt a better attitude towards his mother, for she must surely die at some time. Which interpretation should one take in this particular instance? Perhaps both?

Strangely enough, John M— said he thought his vision of an island paradise was some time in the future. He had no explanation for this; he just 'felt' it. He felt equally convinced that it was not in the past.

Lastly, David H— also thought that his crash into the sea, before 'flying' (stiff, like a corpse?) could be a prediction that he might die by crashing into the sea, being washed up on a beach, and then seeing one form of himself emerge from his dead body to go flying around the countryside and then across the entire continent towards his birthplace before going on to 'somewhere'. At the same time, he was prepared to look upon his vision as a warning, which might be the most optimistic attitude to take. Taking account of all considerations, however, he said he felt convinced that his experience was to take place some time in the future.

So if the procedure by practice enables us to obtain glimpses of the future, or even simply of *possible* future events which we should either prepare for or try to avoid, this would be a further marvel.

Similarity to Normal Subconscious Dreams

Whether one remembers it or not, one dreams several times a night; this is a scientific discovery, or observation, which has been made only within the last few years. Sleep laboratories are now investigating the process of dreaming, at the University of Chicago under Nathaniel Kleitman, and under Dr S. Krippner of the Dream Laboratory at the Community Mental Health Center of Maimonides Medical Centre in Brooklyn, New York—and also all over the rest of the world, in Britain, the Netherlands, France, Russia, China, and even at the University of remote Western Australia. Investigations are being made with new electronic equipment, with the result that some of the information and answers to centuries-old questions have already upset many common beliefs. The notion that we only dream in black-and-white and not in colour was one of the first to be disproved.

Dreams are recorded in the Bible, particularly in the Old Testament, where they were regarded as messages from God; few theologians would claim this for them today. Yet Jacob dreamt of his ladder, Pharaoh of his fat cows and corn being devoured by lean cows and corn, which Joseph eventually interpreted for him as drought years devouring those of rich harvest years. And the Book of Numbers exhorts: 'Hear now my words. If there be a prophet among you, I the Lord will make myself known unto him in a vision, and will speak to him in a dream.'

Through the ages, prophets and saints have had 'divine inspirations' in visions or dreams, even if they were awake at the time, but have rarely experienced them during the usual activity of day—or night, for that matter.

The Jews and Egyptians believed dreams to be of great importance; and certainly their civilizations were far more advanced mentally or psychologically than even we are today after mankind's dreadful relapse during the Dark and Middle Ages, and from which, now, we may be only just emerging.

Both Egyptians and Greeks believed that dreams could help a sick or troubled person, and both practised 'dream incubation'. This was merely a matter of giving a sleep- and/or dream-inducing medicine, like a modern psychedelic drug such as LSD 25; at that time it was probably the prevalent hallucinatory mushroom, or mescalin from a common cactus, or opium from poppies. The 'patient' then spent the night in a temple where he was supposed to have a dream which would help him overcome his problem. Much of modern psychiatry is little different. About 350 B.C., Aristotle, trying to overcome much of the superstition which did, and still does, surround dreams, pointed out that they influenced a person's mood for the ensuing day, and that they could reveal symptoms of illness before these were even noticed by the so-called alert, or aware, waking mind. Two hundred years later, about 150 B.C., the Roman, Artemidorus, spent a lifetime recording and interpreting dreams for his book *Oneirocritica* or *The Interpretation of Dreams*, which remained in use for sixteen centuries. The same title was used by Freud for his work on the subject some 2,000 years later. So Freud's 'discoveries' were not quite new or unknown. Moreover they were limited by his conviction that all dreams were due to repressed childhood desires and that all such desires were sexual. Yet can a 'sick' mind needing help be expected to be well enough to fabricate dreams with images and messages sufficiently inspired to make that sick mind better?

Jung concluded that some dreams at least contained insights outside ordinary experience, and ideas or images which the dreamer could not possibly have acquired or learned only during his own lifetime. And so he conceived 'dream symbols from generation to generation' which could be likened to ontogenesis, or even ontology (the science of the principles of 'pure being', that part of metaphysics which treats of the nature and very essence of things). At the same time he conceived what appears to be the very opposite, yet perhaps is just the other side of the coin, or what he called a 'collective unconscious', or perhaps a kind of phylogenesis. Suffice it to say that man's loftiest and most complicated ideas *about* his ideas, or at least those of which he is aware, reach the conscious mind from the unconscious. From this it seems natural to assume that it is the dream, or subconscious, that has the higher reality than the conscious. It was Jung who named the two archetypes of the 'wise old man', standing for all that is spiritual or creative, and the 'earth mother', standing for all that is practical and down-to-earth, which, to me, defines precisely the two minds—the subconscious and the conscious—their differences from each other, and therefore their intended roles.

I think I should attempt here to define 'consciousness', apart from its being, of course, a state of wakefulness which enables us to focus our will, but only in a very restricted way, on a single, infinitesimal facet of existence at any one time. With the help of 'memory' (the tiny fragment of the subconscious permitted to the conscious) it controls our actions, preventing them from becoming chaotic. Thus it enables us to live in the dimensions of height, width and depth, and in the less perceptible and tangible dimension of time, along with its probable twin, mathematics.

Man, in his wakeful or conscious mind, regards both time and mathematics from the much-too-narrow confines of his own focus and will. He uses a fragment of memory, and overlooks his enormous reserves of true memory and possible, indeed probable, ontogenesis in his subconscious. For instance, I have always been rather suspicious about algebra: it makes so much of mathematical formulae, and is itself much used for the derivation of formulae in the enormous mathematical demands now being made upon mankind for its conception and exploration of space. In other words, I suspect that we regard our mathematical needs from too narrow a focus, and therefore from too narrow a concept, with so much seeming to resolve on the concept of zero, or nothing, rather than on infinity, or everything. I feel that we should never lose sight of the flow or continuum between the two, between nothing and infinity, rather than merely using somewhat primitive concepts of negative and positive, or minus and plus, which lead us no further than to the recent concept, in our efforts to counterbalance our 'realization' of matter, with a premised concept of *anti*-matter.

After centuries since early history of being ignored, the dream (or subconscious or spiritual part of our minds) is only now again being regarded by that wakeful or conscious and therefore confined part of our minds; yet it is the dream which should lead us to assume that there must be as much of, if not more than, the spiritual in the physical. Its obverse, or our presumption of matter being purely physical, is now obviously inadequate and perhaps far from true, and therefore is incorrect.

An easy example of this may be the similarity of the work of such musicians as Bach and Mozart with mathematics. Another way to explain the possible fallacy of man's mathematical conceptions is in his easy acceptance of minus quantities for hypothetical, yet nevertheless seemingly practical, mathematical problems, such as taking thirty apples from twenty apples to give a result of minus ten apples. And yet we all know that it is simply not physically possible to have 'minus ten apples'. This most of us can accept as being impossible, yet we can also accept the mathematical circumstance of taking thirty dollars from twenty dollars and having a minus of, or an overdraft for, ten dollars.

When this minus concept is applied to, say, temperatures and physical gravities—let alone the convoluted distances of space—this contradictory if simple concept is used for the construction of mathematical formulae, even though that simple consideration of the square-foot of a minus quantity (or anti-matter?) is unable, in our concept, to remain a pure minus quantity as the two minus quantities cancel each other out to become a plus (or *plus*-matter?) quantity.

Yet, if only because man has so far discovered nothing, not even a vacuum, that is *less* than nothing, is it not by starting with a false if conveniently hypothetical premise of a minus quantity (which in actuality must be a plus quantity, to a low degree, and is only a minus quantity in man's false concept of measurement) that man is unable to arrive at so many of the true solutions which still elude him? Indeed, doesn't he arrive at only *false* conclusions, which lead him only further into chaos with his technological advancement?

Why have I floundered through all this which is, quite obviously, beyond my grasp? Only to point out that what we regard as a kind of solid reality may suddenly be found to have skidded from under our feet. It should then be obvious that the spiritual or intangible qualities, call them what you will, which appear to us in our subconscious should also be taken into consideration in our conscious or waking life.

But now to return to the phenomena of dreams and dreaming.

Both conscious and unconscious activities of the brain are accompanied by electrical impulses and chemical action; the electrical impulses can be studied by the attachment of electrodes to the head. Through these electrodes infinitesimal electric currents in the brain (and the even more infinitesimal changes in those currents) can be detected. They are amplified to something of the order of a million times. Electro-encephalograms chart these signals producing what are literally 'head pictures'.

These machines are also used to measure the rapid eye and eye-muscle movements which have been observed to take place during various periods of sleep. By waking the sleeper when the movements occur, it has been discovered that they happen when the experimentee is dreaming. Rapid eye movements occur in newborn babies and very old people, and so we now know that we dream from the time of birth (if not while we are still in the womb) until the day—or perhaps even the moment—of death. Indeed, a baby spends most of its time sleeping and naturally spends much of that time dreaming. A normal mature adult spends approximately a quarter of his sleeping time dreaming, and the period diminishes to about a fifth of sleeping time in old age.

My experimentees' conscious dreams were always accompanied by the same rapid eye and eye-muscle movements; but, not being a scientist myself, I was unable to use an electroencephalogram to measure them.

How important dreams are to our psyches and states of mind has only begun to be investigated scientifically since the mid-1950s. It seems extraordinary to me that a phenomenon known to man for thousands of years should have been ignored by science for so long. But now that it has become possible to detect when a sleeper is dreaming by his rapid eye movements (or REM), it is, of course, also possible to wake him in the middle of a dream, and furthermore to discover the effect of the denial of dreaming.

When this was done with groups of volunteers, it was found that it took only five nights without dreaming—not without sleep—for the volunteers to become jittery and anxious. Some found it difficult to concentrate and others gave up the experiment in sheer panic. Other groups were awakened the same number of times as the first sets of volunteers, but without interruption or denial of their *dream*-sleep, and the second group had none of the psychological difficulties of those who were denied dreams. Some volunteers went as long as fifteen nights without dream sleep, but they tried more and more frequently to dream, until eventually they tried all the time to dream and had to be awakened constantly. When the awakenings were stopped and the volunteers allowed to sleep normally, they spent very much more time in dreaming than usual, and continued to do so until the lost dream-time had been made up.

These early experiments, now substantiated to a very great extent, show that it is as necessary for man to dream as to eat and drink, and perhaps even more necessary than for him to sleep without the periods of dreaming. We must dream to be psychologically healthy. A truly healthy person has succeeded in blending his outer and inner selves; and to do this, he must dream.

This, then, may be another use of the Christos procedure: for people who must remain conscious and responsive to danger for long stretches of time (for example, on space flights), it is a way of achieving the necessary dream-time. Dreams can, of course, be induced by LSD and other psychedelic drugs; but they hardly leave the recipient of such drugs conscious, let alone aware and capable of action. At the same time they do a great amount of physical damage to the brain.

One last point, which should be of concern to theologians and all religious people, is that these experiments prove what many laymen have known for a very long time—that dreams, and REM (rapid-eye-movement) sleep, are characteristic of all mammals, not only of human beings. Those who say 'The cat [or dog, or the horse, etc.] is dreaming,' perhaps adding, 'It must be a nightmare, poor thing', or else 'It must be a good dream he's having!' are quite right. And if so—and if dreams are of the subconscious, or the spirit, or the 'soul'—then the regret which some human beings feel that such animals do not have souls and therefore are not considered able to 'go to heaven' can perhaps now be assuaged. It may be even greater consolation to know that reptiles, such as turtles and snakes, etc., do *not* dream, but I have heard of no experiments carried out on insects.

There is another consideration that can arise from the consciously induced dream, and that is Freud's discovery that telepathy seems to work more often during sleep than in times of consciousness; also that the incidence of dreaming an event, which turns out to have happened in reality at the very time of the dream is very frequent indeed, just as predictive dreams are also fairly common. With the Christos procedure, therefore, though I have not yet encountered it with the mere two dozen or so experiments I have made so far, it could be possible to bring telepathy, or extra-sensory perception, and even predictive abilities or clairvoyance, to very many human beings. Australian aborigines already have this ability, and still practise it, so perhaps this ability has always belonged to mankind; until now, however, most other races have been too preoccupied with the functional, the practical, and the mercenary aspects of life.

Revelations of Past Lives?

It is perhaps fortunate that two of these experiences were my own (Chapters 1 and 7), otherwise I feel convinced I would still be the sceptic I was when I first heard of this procedure and the claims made for it. Now I am forced to admit that the sheer detail revealed in such experiences, setting aside the marvel of the imagery and reality of form and colour, is beyond the imagination of a novelist or even, perhaps, of possibly the most imaginative writer of all, the author of science-fiction. Even for an imagination capable of such detail, there just isn't time for so much to be 'faked' or concocted. And even if there had been the time for this with some experimentees, who would have needed to have intelligence quotients in the genius range (which my experimentees did not have), they would have been bound to trip up over some detail or other somewhere. Yet this never happened.

In my own particular case, the periods of time of my possible past lives are quite easy to assess, yet I also admit that they could be purely messages from my subconscious to tell me, as a psychoanalyst would, how marvellous the alphabet is for enabling man to convey his every thought far beyond the power of the much more restricted hieroglyphics. (Hieroglyphics remained so restricted for many centuries until the Egyptians, for example, evolved phonetic hieroglyphics; the *sound* of a word could be represented and still works out, even if the meaning of it has long since been lost.)

My second experience, of course, strongly substantiated this by showing me the sheer marvel of language—a revelation which gave me a childlike sense of wonder and also told me, perhaps, that I must leave my present environment, where there is an indifference towards writers amounting, indeed, to hostility, which makes it almost impossible to work here.

If I find that I am once again able to write after several years of being denied this ability and, particularly, if I find that I have regained the sheer enjoyment and the very reason for living that the ability used to give me, then I must also heed the other message of the second experience—to remove myself from this hostile environment to another. Was it, then, purely chance that I should have envisaged a foreign people whose language I must learn, and who had faces like those depicted in Van Gogh's 'The Potato Eaters'? Is it just a further coincidence that my assistant-companion should happen to be Dutch and that his mother should offer us her house in the Netherlands to continue our work in an environment which, in the 1960s, I had indeed found inspiring to a degree I have never experienced in Australia?

It all seems fairly obvious. But if this is the meaning of the experience, does it exclude the possibility that it is a revelation of a past life, perhaps even of several previous incarnations of my eternal self, which has to progress from primitive incarnations to that ultimate greatness that some instinct informs us is our sole purpose for living?

The claim made for the Christos Experiment is that the procedure can produce visions of past lives which are pertinent to the one we are at present living and, more particularly, to problems which may be confronting us in our present life. (This would be applicable to my own two experiences.) It is also claimed that if the experimentee does not understand the message of his experience, or does not see what he should do about his present predicament, he will return to the same past life or vision until he does understand and know what to do.

Does this, then, apply to the two so-similar 'lives' (Chapters 3 and 6) in both of Ray's Norwegian experiences? He himself says so, and declares that he now feels convinced of this. He wants to try once more, as he also feels that he was unready for the experiment. Furthermore, knowing what he knows now about it, he wants to have the procedure conducted at a much more leisurely pace. He says, 'I think you must be given time just to think, and talk, and describe yourself—and I think then you can wander.' (Quoted verbatim from his tape.) He feels convinced that he saw himself as he must previously have been many centuries ago.

His wife Joy has the same conviction. And after the incredible amount of detail which I have recounted verbatim, is it any wonder that she should do so? Yet her two experiences (Chapters 4 and 14) also show the conflict she has always had over religion, particularly with Roman Catholicism, since her ancestry is partly (probably largely) Jewish. This explains, perhaps, her second experience with 'Jesus', but at an age when his whereabouts and activities are not known. For she was quite adamant that he was twenty-three—too old for the days of his youth which *are* known, and before the few years, from about the age of thirty until his death at thirty-three, which make up the brief period when most is known about him.

At the same time, she became a man—and this is perhaps wishful thinking. She has often said that she wishes she were a man and, as like so many women, that she wants to be one 'in my *next* life'. How many men wish they could be women? If we should be reincarnated in order to develop our spiritual selves—and what other self could possibly be worth developing?—is it then some form of punishment, or more arduous circumstance, to be incarcerated in the body of a woman rather than that of a man? Shades of Virginia Woolf's *Orlando*! But what shades for philosophers and theosophers to consider!

Julie W—'s experience as a young American girl about a hundred years ago (Chapter 16, Part 2) has so little else in it that she and her husband, such sceptics at the commencement of the experiment, as most are, feel now that it can only be a glimpse of a past life. Certainly if she was then compelled to work in boy's clothes (though she was permitted to sleep as a girl), she is now always carefully and strikingly but femininely dressed. What circumstances of that life, however, could possibly have pertained to this one? In her present life her father is dead and her mother has remarried, and she is on excellent terms with her stepfather; whereas, in her 'past life', it was her mother who was dead, and she was on far from excellent terms with the housekeeper, who was mistress of the house as well as her father's mistress. She says she wants to try the experiment again, 'to see more', and perhaps this is one case where a repetition is necessary.

Richard B—'s Roman 'orgy' (Chapter 13) he found immediately applicable to his present life; and yet was it necessary for his or any psyche to take him so far back in history, and in such explicit detail, merely to convey so obvious a point? Since making that experiment, his present life seems already to be both 'reordered' and 'put into order', as though whatever message might have been conveyed by the experience had been received 'loud and clear' and the appropriate action taken. Yet he, too, says he wants to make the experiment again, although he expressed it as wanting 'to have the experience again'.

Next there is Jim McA—'s sojourn in medieval Austria (the first part of Chapter 17) culminating in suicide from a cliff-ledge into impenetrable fog below; he suddenly saw himself transposed back into his own present body and looking up at his previous body while it became increasingly diminutive, instead of larger, as it descended towards him, until finally, as a mere speck, it fell and disappeared into his present mind. If this were a warning against any suicidal tendencies, then his present psyche seems to have taken heed of such warning long before the experiment. But if it were a warning against further aimless wanderings, or taking 'a trip' in the literal sense of travelling the world, then he has disregarded this message by already setting off to cross Australia and return, hitch-hiking and working wherever he can. After this, he plans to go west to Africa, north to Europe once more, then still further west before returning home to the United States.

If Jim McA—'s revelation was to show me that no harm can come to an experimentee's present body, or mind, no matter what may befall him during his experience of a possible past, then it seems hardly fair to him to have endured so much for someone else's benefit. Perhaps I shall have the opportunity of taking him for another experience to see if any further meaning was to have been conveyed.

But there is no reason—no reason whatsoever—why someone else shouldn't take Jim for another trip. Or, has it just occurred to me, is it possible to 'go' entirely by one's self? Whatever happens, I shall never forget the way Jim looked and spoke when he said that, in all his travels and so many 'weirdo' experiences, he had never encountered anything to be compared with this experience.

And there is Ruby B— (Chapter 15), whose experience is to me the most astounding of all. She is still convinced that she was a bird in that past life of hers, and an albatross at that, always gliding over cold southern oceans, though perhaps she could have been a storm or stormy petrel, a Mother Carey's chicken, that dusky seabird which rarely lands except to lay its eggs and which has the smallest webbed feet known in birds. And if the mind has baulked at the prospect of our indeed having had past lives with several incarnations, then it may baulk even more at the prospect of perhaps having once been a bird, or some kind—*any* kind—of animal. And it must find it even harder merely to consider some future life having to be spent as some kind of mammal other than a human being. And yet, *is* it so incredible? My own mother, long before she died, used often to say that in her next life she wanted to be a seal, she loved the ocean so, but would nevertheless still like to be able to set foot—or tail—on land occasionally.

All through time there have been people and references to people who have believed in reincarnation, from the early

Egyptians to such a practical man as General Patton. And there is, too, Londoner Mrs Rosemary Brown who for years has written down the music 'dictated' to her by dead composers, from Bach to Debussy; Liszt appeared to her when she was a child saying he would return when she was grown up and would then communicate music to her; all of this is recounted in her book *Unfinished Symphonies*. In it she also says that many people have asked her why, without any musical knowledge, she should have been chosen for this duty and privilege; she replied that she herself asked the same question of Liszt, and received the reply that it was because she had volunteered for this duty 'in an earlier life'. Yet just as Rosemary Brown wrote of the inspirational dreams that led her to continue writing the music of so many composers, one of those composers, Mozart, himself wrote of the frequent 'creative' dreams which occur to so many creative artists—composers, writers, painters, sculptors—as follows:

'The whole, though it be long, stands almost complete and finished in my mind, so that I can survey it, like a fine picture or a beautiful statue, at a glance. Nor do I hear in my imagination the parts successively, but I hear them, as it were, all at once. What a delight this is I cannot tell! All this inventing, this producing, takes place in a lively dream.' And, 'What has been thus produced I do not easily forget, and this is perhaps the best gift I have my Divine Maker to thank for.'

The poet Samuel Taylor Coleridge recorded a similar experience when he wrote 'Kubla Khan'. Before going to sleep he had read from a book that 'here the Khan Kubla commanded a palace to be built, and a stately garden thereunto. And thus ten miles of fertile ground were enclosed within a wall'. In about three hours of dreaming, after having taken a medicine when feeling unwell, he saw images rise up before him which suggested words as though they were expressing themselves, about two or three hundred lines of them already composed for him by his 'inner mind'; these he commenced to write down quickly as soon as he awoke. However, he had written only the first ten lines or so, word for word as he had 'seen' them, when a messenger interrupted him, after which he could no longer exactly remember the lines he had dreamed. But his *memory* of the dream enabled him to construct a finished poem.

Robert Louis Stevenson often used dreams for his work, particularly childhood nightmares. In one dream he had led a double life, and this gave him the idea for *Dr Jekyll and Mr Hyde*. Later, nightmares gave way to dreams of journeying, and from these came his *Travels with a Donkey*.

Graham Greene in his *A Sort of Life* says that dreams have always had an importance for him—'the finest entertainment known, and given rag cheap'. Two novels and several short stories emerged from his dreams, he writes. Sometimes he had 'hints of what is called by the difficult name of extra-sensory perception' and gives as an example a night when he was five years old and dreamt of a shipwreck; it was the night of the 'Titanic' disaster. Over many years now, some of Graham Greene's novels have been uncanny for appearing just prior to some catastrophe in the country where they are set: *The Quiet American* in Indo-China (now Vietnam), *Our Man in Havana* in Cuba, *A Burnt-Out Case* in the Belgian Congo, *The Comedians* in Haiti. His is a sense of timeliness before the fact, which is sometimes shared by Australia's Morris West.

Should I quote myself? Why not, since I suppose that I *have* already written a good deal. One longish short story, the last and title story of a volume, I dreamt in its entirety: *The Road to Nowhere*. In a travel book, *The Land that Sleeps*, I recounted the visualization of a 'sort of poem' which I saw word for word; I had also seen the layout I used in the book, with its *vertical* title of *To Popes and Politicians*, as I slept near the beautiful yet at times quite terrifying Dale's Gorge in the north of Western Australia.

I was in the Lebanon, of all places, when I dreamt an entire play—scene for scene and almost, I think, word for word—which, when awake, I felt all the time was being *dictated* to me from some inner or supernatural plane, by the protagonist herself, who was none other than the late Marilyn Monroe on whom I based the play, *Turn on the Heat*. The only novels of the twelve I have written to date which have sprung in their entirety direct from a dream, or an image derived from a dream, were *O Loneliness* and *Flight to Landfall*, which were set, in both dream and novel, in Western Australia with, admittedly, Dutch connections or references, and actual Dutch characters in *Flight to Landfall*.

Previous to this, the whole novel did not appear in dreams

but sections of it did and led to the writing of my first fantasy, *A Change of Mind*. Another, which through illness and injury has been eluding me for years, is now under way after having been dreamt, originally in Rimini on the Adriatic coast, but also recurrently and frequently in other parts of the world. As the setting of this dream is the Netherlands, it is yet another reason why I must return there to write the book. I have tentatively entitled it *Alicia*; one section of it, which was *dreamed* some time previously on its own, has already appeared as a longish story called 'The Ice Yacht' in *The Road to Nowhere*.

As Erich von Däniken writes in his *Return to the Stars*, referring to the inspirational dreams of two scientists (like August Kekulé's dream of benzine's molecular structure being in the form of a snake swallowing its own tail):

> I believe that what these two brilliant natural scientists 'dreamed' already rested on the basis of their 'age-old' knowledge. In the beginning there is always an idea (or a dream) that has to be proved in practice. I think it quite likely that one day the molecular geneticists, who already know how the genetic code functions, will also find out how much—and even which—information was programmed on the punched cards of our life by unknown intelligences. It sounds fantastic, but one fine day we might even discover by which code-word a specific piece of knowledge for a specific purpose can be summoned up from the primitive memory.
>
> In my opinion cosmic memories penetrated more and more strongly into our consciousness in the course of man's evolution. They encouraged the birth of new ideas, which had already been realized in practice at the time of the visit by the 'gods'. At certain fortunate moments the barriers separating us from the primitive memory fall. Then the driving forces brought to light, again by the stored-up knowledge, become active in us.
>
> Is it only a coincidence that printing and clockmaking, that the car and the aeroplane, that the law of gravity and the functioning of the genetic code, were invented and 'discovered' almost simultaneously at different times in different parts of the world?

Since the remote past we have all lived in an evolutionary spiral that carries us irresistibly into the future, into a future which I am convinced has already been the past; not a human past, but the past of the 'gods' which is at work in us and will become the present one day. We are still waiting for definite scientific proof. But I *believe* in the power of those chosen spirits to whom a subtle selective mechanism is given that will one day release to them the information stored up in the dim past about realities that have existed. Until that happy day dawns, I support Teilhard de Chardin when he says: 'I believe in science, but has science ever taken the trouble to consider the world except from the outside of things?'*

To yet another and a far different part of the world, and a very different way of life: the Biami Papuans of Western Papua (one of the most primitive races of people in our modern world, who carry woven bags containing the bones of their dead ancestors) claim that they are able to talk with their dead during tribal rites or seances. They also believe in a form of telepathy among themselves, and say that every death in their community contributes new knowledge to a communal 'spirit mind' which the spirits of those who have died, or 'passed on', preserve for those who are still living. An Australian film crew has filmed a tribe of these people whereas, only five or six years ago, they would probably have been killed with arrows and eaten. The locality of this tribe, and therefore of the film, is Obeimi, about two days' walk from the tiny Nomad River air strip. The area is one of the poorest parts of Papua New Guinea, and the Biami Papuans have developed a struggling society, as has the Australian aboriginal, whose existence depends on a bare minimum of food. Both races are suspicious of outsiders and steeped in mysticism and death cults. The film will deal not only with their daily functional routines, but will also show activities relating to their spiritual beliefs and supernatural attitudes to their environment.

One could go on endlessly, from past to present, from the primitive to our so-called civilization. But I think this is enough. Just as I do not want to recount 200 dreams and their interpretations as the Chester Beatty papyrus does, I also do not want

* Erich von Däniken, *Return to the Stars* (Souvenir Press, London, 1970).

to list 200 subjects convinced of their reincarnation. After all, such a belief is a fairly common phenomenon.

What I do want to do is to have this book, or mere record, made available to readers as quickly as possible. For though I may not yet be entirely convinced that we do indeed see past lives by following the Christos procedure, I am nevertheless convinced that a great deal is achieved through it which, to my amazement, has apparently not been achieved before. Alternatively, if it has been achieved previously, it has either been discredited or somehow failed to be conveyed to humanity at large.

This may not be so surprising when one considers how little is still known about our subconscious or 'spiritual' selves, or even of our world of dreams, and how only now such a science as parapsychology is making all too tentative investigations into these matters. This could also indicate that—with the tremendous pressure of our technological knowledge being exerted on this one small planet at the present time, and by beings who are in most other respects still astoundingly and even alarmingly primitive—only now has the need for such preternatural knowledge arisen. And perhaps this is why only now are the amazing results from so simple a procedure becoming widely known. That I should be one of the few to whom it has *become* known fills me with both dismay and awe. Yet at the same time I also feel a profound sense of gratitude, mixed with an equally profound sense of duty.

The duty, I feel, is to make so simple a procedure and its results known as soon as possible to as *many* as possible, for I think one does not have to give it much thought to realize the tremendous benefit it can bestow on all mankind.

To the young, already so earnestly bent upon a world-wide search for an inner reality and meaning to life, in what seems increasingly like chaos in the normal *outer* reality, it can be, at best, a revelation, or, at the very least, 'a trip', without resorting either to drugs, to hypnotism, or to any other artificial means of inducement.

To the middle-aged, it can perhaps bring meaning to what for so many seems such a meaningless life, when they see the physical and acquisitive impulses so obviously come to so abrupt an end. Despite the asseverations of those who still claim religious 'faith', they wonder what all their efforts are for as their children become estranged from them, as they even become estranged from each other, and as the so-called practical things of life—economics, politics, the utilitarian and even technological sciences—seem only to resolve into the appalling primitivism of violence and chaos.

To the elderly it can bring a whole new concept of death as merely of passing on 'as though just walking into another room', so that instead of abhorring and fearing death they may now prepare for it as something perhaps even more of a gift, and even more constructive or creative, than is birth. For death may be yet another *form* of birth—into another world, or another plane—or perhaps returned to this one in some other form or other, for some *lifetime* or other, and yet perhaps for merely a moment as well as a whole lifetime for some *lesson* or other. And this could be so that this immeasurably greater part of us, our spiritual selves mostly regarded as merely our subconscious, may develop towards the immeasurable greatness of which it is capable. Such development can be glimpsed in the mere passage of a lifetime, diminutive as this is compared with our practical awareness of time in billions of not just years but of *light-years*, and of which we are only just now beginning to have a mere glimmer, a mere flicker of awareness, but then perhaps from the wrong concept of it.

Yet again, is even this conception of an inner reality so new after all? Apart from St John's (xiv, 2) 'In my Father's house are many mansions', there are also Shakespeare's words from Hamlet to Horatio: 'There are more things in heaven and earth than are dreamt of in your philosophy.' And just over a hundred years ago, Phoebe Cary wrote:

> Nearer my Father's house,
> Where the many mansions be,
> Nearer the great white throne,
> Nearer the crystal sea.

Perhaps we are only now just beginning to discover these 'many mansions', for just as the *common* dream is obviously a natural window to the inner self, it may be that this window also reveals a greater reality than we can at present understand.

I can only agree with Arthur Koestler in his *The Ghost in the Machine* that mankind, if it is not to destroy the world and itself, is in dire need of discovering some 'greater reality'. And it may well be that the construction of man's mind is indeed merely a streak of *sanity* in an otherwise insane 'mechanism', as he considers. But I cannot bring myself to believe that our only hope for salvation lies, as Koestler suggests, in a mere pill, a sort of universal tranquillizer, perhaps, to subdue our insanity; for would that not also subdue the mere streak of *sanity* as well, and perhaps the sanity *before* the *in*sanity? No, I feel that if man is to survive to become the truly noble creature he was intended to be, then he will do so by the enlightenment and resolve of his own free will, through the widening of his conscious focus to a far greater reality than that we know already.

Moreover, if indeed America's B. F. Skinner is right in surmising that man can no longer afford freedom (by which he means an external freedom in man's external world) but must come to live as a 'conditioned being' (John M—'s 'computerized people'?), then perhaps now is indeed the time when man must discover this far greater reality in which, though his conscious life may become little more than an environment of organization and even conditioning to what could be a horrifying degree, he will at the same time discover a freedom beyond bounds through this latest 'window' to be revealed to him.

And this window may only now have been revealed to us to enable us to turn our eyes inwards from the increasing turmoil and dissatisfaction, even disillusionment, with our outside world, so that we may at last begin to view, and find solace and our salvation in, far greater worlds within.

Perth, Western Australia
May–September, 1971

Author's final note in August 1974: My writers' block is obviously over; in the three years since writing this book I have written its sequel, two volumes of short stories, two memoirs, a novella, a screenplay, and two novels, one of over 200,000 words. Currently, five more books are in progress or planned.